# CYCLEPEDIA

# CYCLEPEDIA

*90 Years of Modern Bicycle Design*

Michael Embacher
Photography by Bernhard Angerer
Foreword by Paul Smith
Introduction and bicycle texts by
Martin Strubreiter and Michael Zappe

500 illustrations

Thames & Hudson

# CONTENTS

# FOREWORD

It was at the age of eleven that my world changed from being just a schoolboy living at home to someone who started an adventure with the world of cycling that has never stopped. My parents bought me a pale blue Paramount racing bicycle for my birthday. It was second-hand but in perfect condition, and purchased from a friend of my father's. The friend said that if I ever wanted to join the local cycle club, of which he was a member, and come on rides into the English countryside on a Sunday, I would be very welcome. I did this, and was suddenly aware of the freedom that cycling and the open road gives you – the wind blowing in your face, the sound of the tyres on the roads, and a tremendous sense of achievement when you return home after several hours in the saddle.

I used to keep my bicycle in my bedroom (much to the horror of my mum), but it was always completely immaculate: even after a rainy day I would clean and dry it immediately on returning home. I would sit in bed admiring the colour, the shape, the engineering. In fact, everything about my bike and bicycles has always been very appealing to me.

At the age of twelve I started to race in the schoolboy category, and later went on to become a junior. My best place in a road race was sixth. I never won anything and my cycling finished with a bad accident aged seventeen, which resulted in several months in hospital. After recovering I met up with some new friends from the hospital at the local pub, which by chance was the meeting place of many creative students – studying fashion, architecture, photography, art, graphic design, etc. – from the local art college. Meeting these students changed my life, as that is when I turned my attention to design. The rest, as they say, is history, although cycling has continued to be a hobby and a passion.

It is with this history that I can absolutely identify with the passion of Michael Embacher. What a selection – absolutely fantastic! All shapes, sizes and qualities. The amazing Gazelle Champion Mondial, although produced in the late 1970s, had the general appearance of my first bicycle, and I love the high-tech, ultra-modern Schauff Wall Street and the Sablière with its curved tubes and aluminium frame. To be honest, it's just better to look at the book because words alone cannot describe these terrific cycles.

**Paul Smith**

# ON THE FASCINATION WITH BICYCLES

'When the spirits are low, when the day appears dark, when work becomes monotonous, when hope hardly seems worth having, just mount a bicycle and go out for a spin down the road, without thought on anything but the ride you are taking.' Arthur Conan Doyle, *Scientific American Magazine*, 1896

Without doubt, the bicycle is a sensual and personal object that holds many memories, at many levels. You can probably remember your first bike, the moment when the stabilizers were removed and your worst fall. For many children, riding a bike is the first opportunity to expand their play area, to get away from their parents and pursue the adventures of a wider world.

A bike is above all a means for having fun – no matter your age. It is liberating to feel the wind in your hair as you ride, to feel your physical efforts generating a forward motion, to escape the city's traffic jams or to fly across a frozen lake on an ice bike.[1]

The humble bicycle has the power to create immense anticipation and fill entire nations with pride. Think of famous cycle races such as the Tour de France or the Giro d'Italia, in which thousands of fans make their pilgrimage to the race courses, while millions more watch in awe on roadsides and in front of television screens.

Whether you are a rider, spectator or collector, a lover of design and craftsmanship, a do-it-yourself type or even a professional constructor, the bicycle has avid supporters of every kind. In 2007 the German *Zeit Magazin* (a supplement of broadsheet *Die Zeit*) featured an interview with the chairman of Ferrari, Luca Cordero di Montezemolo. In response to the question of what he most liked to drive in his spare time, he answered, 'I like to cycle'.

Of course, we can also celebrate the bicycle for its environmentally friendly attributes, which perfectly reflect the ever-present concerns for our planet. Powered exclusively by human energy, the bicycle is indisputably the most efficient means of transportation anywhere. An exemplary ecological product, it requires no parking space, produces no exhaust fumes and causes no traffic jams. The average bicycle manoeuvres well and is of a small size, making it the smart option when tackling everyday congestion in urban centres. At the same time, it suits our health-conscious times and facilitates any fitness regime, whether on the streets or in the gym. Because bicycles have had such a positive effect on society and daily life, it is my personal wish to see bicycles become a dominant part of the world's cityscapes.

My fascination with the bicycle is with the simplicity of the idea – efficiently transforming human energy into maximum mobility – and how this translates into design. Although the concept of the two-wheeled human-powered vehicle has existed for more than a century, the bicycle continues to be an incredibly relevant product, constantly redesigned, whose basic principles have withstood the test of time.

The bicycle is one of the most uncompromising constructions I know – artistically and structurally. It requires a lightweight structure (as the rider must drive forward the weight of the machine plus himself), a stable frame (to make it efficient) and extreme engineering precision (to minimize any loss of friction), in addition to aspiring to graceful and elegant aesthetics. Bicycle designers around the world are passionate about their art and craft, expending exhaustive hours in their quest for perfection.

This selection does not attempt to categorize bicycles too prescriptively, or to show them chronologically. It offers instead a broad

Michael Embacher amid
the Embacher Collection.

spectrum of what the bicycle can be and the stories surrounding each model. The playful, experimental and innovate elements of a bicycle are as important as who has ridden them and what roles in history they have played.[2,3,4,5] All the bicycles shown here meet the current accepted definitions. They include racing bikes with exquisite details, folding bicycles with conspicuously clever mechanisms and touring bicycles designed with particular care and attention for longer journeys. Also featured are those bicycles that look extraordinary even if their performance is average, track bikes with no brakes that serve as speed machines, and bicycles that defy categorization. All these bicycles are roadworthy: I have tested each personally with either short rides inside or longer rides outside that are part of my daily routine. Being able to enjoy the lighthearted side of bicycles while experiencing the differences between them is for me an enormous luxury.

Cyclepedia invites you to share my endless enthusiasm for the bicycle and may perhaps inspire you to discover your own passion for bikes. If any of the machines in this book spark in the reader a greater interest or admiration in bicycles, or if it reveals just a little of the personal attention lavished by countless constructors, designers and individuals on every tiny component and detail of the bicycle, never mind the enjoyment brought to its rider (whether a casual cyclist or road-racing hero), the book will have succeeded.

**Michael Embacher**

# A BRIEF HISTORY OF BICYCLE DESIGN

There is no international consensus over who invented the bicycle; indeed all that can be proven is that several versions were concocted, refined and perfected in many different countries at the same time.

A common belief is that the Italian artist and inventor Leonardo da Vinci came up with the model in the 15th century, but drawings attributed to him have been exposed as more recent forgeries. Another claim, this time by the Frenchman Comte de Sivrac, has been proven to be untrue and therefore he could not have presented it in Paris in 1791.

If we want to settle on a likely inventor, then we could name Baron Karl von Drais (1785–1851). In 1815 an Indonesian volcano erupted, changing the climate and affecting crops as far afield as Northern Europe. The resulting famine was severe, with Europeans forced to eat horses – a main source of transportation – for sustenance. To tackle the resulting transport problems, Baron von Drais created a 'dandy horse', on which the rider could propel himself while in a sitting position without any pedals. His first reported ride, in June 1817, was in Mannheim, and it was quickly followed by others. However, although the rider could steer he could not brake, and Drais's machine received a mixed reaction in Germany. In other countries where Baron von Drais presented his invention it was a little more successful, but even so he died in poverty in 1851. The first monument to Drais was unveiled in 1893.

Over the last one hundred years bicycle design has continued to evolve, but all successive versions have been refinements of the original idea. This has not prevented many of them from being astonishing in their success. Innovations have tended to come from constructors who are themselves avid cyclists, rather than engineers who drive to work in their cars or 'outsiders' who want to be at the forefront of an industry. Bicycle design might not have moved on that far, but it is the technologies and new materials that have allowed the components to be revolutionary.

## No feet on the ground: pedals

Powering a vehicle by running may work perfectly well for the Flintstones, but outside the cartoon world new ideas were more practical. Pierre Michaux (1813–83) is considered the inventor of the pedal, even though Philipp Moritz Fischer, an instrument maker from Schweinfurt in Bavaria, took to the bumpy roads with the idea at around the same time. These first cranks were rigidly connected to the front wheel, there was no chain, and anyone holding the handlebars too loosely while pedalling would zigzag along.

Pierre Michaux showcased his 'Michauline' velocipede at the Paris International Exposition in 1867. It was a great success. Those who could afford the Michauline had found a new toy, and the first velocipede societies were founded.

## Roll over wood: steel and rubber

The first velocipedes were heavy and made of cast iron and wood, and the wheels had only iron rings as 'tyres'. In the UK and the

LABOR Spéciale Course

USA they were therefore affectionately known as 'boneshakers', but progress quickly corrected this. James Starley (1830–81) from Coventry in the UK looked to the steel industry, and so steel frames, rims and spokes were developed – the tender beginnings of lightweight construction.

The rubber industry was responsible for the comfort. It first supplied solid rubber tyres, heavy but puncture-proof, but in 1888 John Boyd Dunlop invented the pneumatic tyre – and with it the flat tyre from which we still suffer today.

### High wheel (at the front, at least)

On account of the new materials, the fixed-drive front wheels were manufactured in a significantly larger size, and larger front wheels also increased the speeds. After all, one crank revolution strictly meant one revolution of the wheel and there was still no talk of gears. Moving at 20 to 25 kilometres (12 to 15 miles) per hour was suddenly possible. The front wheels grew to over 150 centimetres (59 inches) in diameter, while the rear wheels became smaller and were demoted to the status of mere supporting wheels. And so the penny farthing turned the corner into the 1880s.

### Sitting lower, aiming high: the safety bicycle

Just getting on the penny farthing was difficult (anyone who imagines having to climb a ladder is not entirely wrong), but it was even more difficult getting down – particularly when something unexpected suddenly got in the way. Most people who ride penny farthings seriously these days, for example, in competitions or displays, have at some point ended up on a car roof, and there would have been an equivalent likely ending in the 1880s. Every obstacle before the front wheel was an opportunity to fall over on to your head, and even ridiculous inventions such as safety handlebars (which detached themselves in the event of a fall, tumbling head first to the ground with the rider) barely helped matters.

The situation was only improved with the introduction of a chain drive. Gradually the rear wheel came to be driven, and little by little the two wheels became the same size and the cyclist once more sat close to the ground. Evolution saw to it that in 1895 the penny farthing was discontinued, while the 'low' bicycle (or 'safety' bicycle) rode away into the future, initially as a piece of sports equipment and a plaything for the rich.

It still had to win general acceptance and it did this through sporting success; on the roads, it had the horse to compete with. On 29–30 June 1893 the horse was defeated on the long-distance Vienna–Berlin race, which was an amazing 580 kilometres long. Joseph Fischer cycled the route in 31 hours, beating Count Starhemberg's horseback attempt a year earlier, which had taken 71 hours and 35 minutes. There would be no serious competition from the car for a long time yet; even in 1900, a Bollée car still took 26 hours to drive from Vienna to Berlin – not much of an improvement on the bicycle even at big distances.

### From corsets to culottes: women on bicycles

At this point it was still only men who rode bicycles. At the end of the 19th century ideas of morality were rather simple, and a bicycle seemed far removed from women's traditional role. In 1891, a bishop compared the idea of women cycling with that of riding a broomstick, and doctors – who had almost certainly never ridden a bicycle – advised women against cycling for 'medical reasons'. Any woman wanting to ride a bike either had to do so disguised as a man or opt for a tricycle which could also be ridden with a wide skirt.

It was only slowly that women began to dare to ride penny farthings and safety bikes, and the issue of clothing was not all that difficult to overcome. Culottes or 'bloomers', compatible with cycling but relatively modest in appearance, provided a temporary solution, although real trousers for women were still a long way off. With this newfound freedom, the daring women cyclists also discarded their corsets, and liberty and emancipation were slowly given room to breathe.

### Onwards and upwards: the arrival of gears

The first derailleur – a mechanism for moving the chain from one sprocket to another to change gears – was the 'Gradient', devised in the in around 1895. Shortly afterwards came the hub gears, with those produced by Sturmey-Archer proving a British national treasure for decades. These days, however, a German shifting hub fills that niche: the Rohloff Speedhub 500/14 with 14 gears.[1]

The derailleur was developed from around 1910 onwards, more often in France than elsewhere. The dialogue between the different systems was intense and had its fair share of absurdities.[2] The first parallelogram gear-shift mechanism produced in high quantities, however, came from Italy. Tullio Campagnolo had learned well from observing the first pioneers and from 1950 his 'Gran Sport' gear mechanism[3] became the benchmark, although its price was far above the standard. With numerous refinements (aluminium in place of steel, and countless changes to the smaller details), it was sold as the 'Nuovo Record' model up to the mid-1980s.[4]

The first gear mechanisms were incidentally more popular with touring cyclists, whereas racing cyclists saw them as an unfair dilution of pure man-power.[5] Gear mechanisms were not allowed in the Tour de France until 1937.

W. & R. BAINES V.S 37

BOB JACKSON Super Legend

compact cranks), and used aluminium for the brakes, cranks, lights, mudguards, handlebars, stems and pedals. These refinements soon became standard, and international commercial success followed. Constructors such as Paul Charrel,[6] Jo Routens and Lionel Brans became famous for the quality of their bicycles, and René Herse and Alex Singer became the most famous of all. Herse and Singer produced not only beautiful frames with braze-ons, but also entire bicycles with every component integrated.

### The idea that came in from the cold: Campagnolo's quick-release mechanism

Before the randonneur competitions, the history of gear shifting was dotted with simpler methods with the most straightforward being the reverse hub. A second, larger sprocket was attached to the rear wheel hub on the left-hand side, and at the foot of a steep ascent, the rear wheel was simply turned around.[5, 7]

So that no spanner would be needed for this purpose, wing nuts were invented. They worked perfectly well until 11 November 1927, when Tullio Campagnolo was riding in a cycling race on the Croce d'Aune, a mountain pass in the Dolomites. In the driving snow at the summit, his fingers proved simply too numb to release the wing nuts. Campagnolo's frustration bore another invention, and he eliminated the problem in 1930, when he was granted a patent for a quick-release mechanism. In 1933 he founded his company, and in 1940 hired his first employees.

### Beyond a joke: funny frames from the UK

Astonishingly, the British – traditionally endearing in their quirkiness – never had the idea of mounting the drive on the left-hand side. Instead they created refreshing alternatives to the diamond frame from the 1930s onwards, with every company completely convinced that its invention was the future of frame building.

### A new way to travel: randonneur bicycles and the best constructors

In the early 20th century cycle races were sheer luxury, with most bicycles being used instead for everyday purposes and sometimes for touring. Riding a bike meant not having to travel along rails, and unlike horses a bike did not need oats, nor did it emit any bad smells or mess.

Most bicycle tourists (cyclotouristes) went to cycle in France, and so the first practical tests were also there. In 1901 brakes were tested in the mountains (with shocking results, as most contemporary brakes were unable to cope). Experiments with gear mechanisms were carried out as early as 1913, and in the 1930s amateurs building single prototypes had evolved into organized constructor championships. The best frame constructors aimed to produce the lightest, most robust and fastest touring bicycles.

The finest randonneur bicycles were around 7 kilograms in weight. They possessed between 8 and 15 gears with two or three front chain rings (their difference in size anticipated the modern

Hetchins, with the curved rear-frame stays (curly or vibrant stays)[8] or Bates, with the double-curve fork (Diadrant fork) and tubes which were thickened in the middle (Cantiflex tubes), did not stray far from the diamond frame. Others, however, such as Baines with its Flying Gate,[7] Waller with the Kingsbury and Paris with its Galibier, wanted to overhaul bicycle history with radically new forms.

This overhaul came first of all in the price. Many of these alternative frames were expensive to produce and thus out of the question for mass production, leaving only the small producers involved. The designs were usually intended to make the frame lighter and more rigid. However, the effect was mainly in the imagination – although this could have a powerful impact in cycling where the mind is closely connected to the legs. The heyday of 'strange' frames came after World War II when many small bicycle producers were pushing their way into the market in an attempt to share in the bicycle boom. They felt these extravagant frame designs would satisfy the customers. In reality the only frames to survive were those that could be brazed (soldered) with just a little extra effort: the Bates and Hetchins.[8, 9]

## Conflict and the car boot: folding bicycles

The bicycle had slowly changed its position in society. In the very early years they were possessions for the wealthy, but when the first cars took to the streets, the nobility had a new toy. Mass-production techniques made the bicycle accessible to the wider public. Second-hand bicycles slowly became affordable, followed even by brand-new ones, and workers' sports clubs were set up. Up until long after World War II, the bicycle was what the car is today: the transport for the masses.

The military had noticeably little to do with the bicycle,[10] but its career was not entirely without military action. As early as the Franco-Prussian War in 1870–71, it was employed in the courier

T&C Pocket Bici

LOTUS Sport 110

service, and later military units were even mobilized using them. This prompted the invention of the folding bicycle at the end of the 19th century, and in 1910 the German 'Colibri' became the first folding bike to use small 20-inch wheels. Designed specifically for hunters or soldiers, placing the feet on the ground would immediately turn the bicycle into a stable tripod for shooting.

However, it was not until the age of a fully motorized society in the 1960s that folding bikes really became popular.[11, 12, 13, 14] The idea was for them to sit in the car boot taking up little space but ready to be used, although in reality they tended to sit forgotten in the cellar. In parallel with the first fashion for folding bicycles Alex Moulton, inventor of the suspension for the Austin Mini, experimented in the UK with his reinvention of the bicycle with small wheels and full suspension.[3, 15] The trend in folding bikes therefore took inspiration from a bike that (with the exception of Moulton's Stowaway model) could not be folded.

So the bicycle reached its career low: a stopgap for whenever you were not in the car. The quality and beauty of touring bicycles had declined and, unsurprisingly, so had the sales figures. Only the racing bike was able to flourish in its niche – a situation that did not change until, at the beginning of the 1970s, some eccentrics put a bicycle on a mountain.

### Back to the game: mountain bikes

The mountain bike was invented by many individuals at around the same time, but it is generally attributed to Gary Fisher. An active ambassador for the mountain bike even today, Fisher can still ride young cyclists off the track in marathons.

Gary Fisher had his first success in cycle racing, but from 1968 he was banned from the American Cycling Association due to his long hair, and was only readmitted in 1972. From 1973 it took him and his friends (including Joe Breeze[16] and Charlie Kelly) into off-road terrain. They modified Schwinn Cruiser frames from the 1930s using particularly robust components. Because of their weight, the bikes had to arrive in a pick-up truck to California's Mount Tamalpais, in order to race down into the valley along gravel paths. At the bottom of the trail, the coaster brake hubs had become so hot that the grease melted and ran out, and had to be refilled again. And so the early downhill races got their name: the repack race.

### Form follows form: the triumph of design

The mountain bike shook technical progress from its decades-old lethargy, but this progress also left its mark through unmistakable design and by pointing extravagantly towards a lighter, more beautiful future.

It was then that the new materials of future frames arrived on the scene. Aluminium,[17] previously a side branch in bicycle history prone to twisting, became a broad, light, rigid mainstay in the form of an oversized tube. In its shadow, titanium[15] celebrated a brief flash of the finest non-corrosive enthusiasm, before it was edged out by carbon moulding. Carbon frames (hollow bodies that could be moulded to any shape) then became available to a wide playing field of designers, and the monocoque[18, 19, 20] broke the diamond mould of frame design. A variety of innovative shapes, never seen before, inspired designers around the world. Suddenly even folding bikes could be rigid, beautiful and fast. Steel could happily fulfil a role that previously had barely been open to it – the graceful alternative for friends of slender, fine frame building, for devotees of ornately filed lugs.

And so we arrive at the present time, and with it the very heart of this book.

*Michael Zappe and Martin Strubreiter*

# VIALLE VÉLASTIC
## WHAT'S IN A NAME?

**VARIETY**
URBAN, CURIOSITY

**COUNTRY**
FRANCE

**DATE**
1925

**WEIGHT**
17.3 KG (38.1 LB)

**FRAME**
VARNISHED STEEL, ADJUSTABLE HEIGHT

**GEARS**
1

**BRAKES**
RIM ROD BRAKE

**TYRES**
26 IN. WIRED

The ideas that later paved the way for the Breezer Beamer (see page 56) were introduced on a bicycle as early as 1925. The Vélastic from the Vialle brothers and their Établissements Industriels des Cycles Élastiques of France was said, as the newspaper advertisements claimed, to make cycling as comfortable as sitting in an armchair. It was even supposed to be possible to ride down a kerb without noticing the drop.

Even when you strip away the usual hyperbole of advertising, the impression that remains of the Vélastic is one of comfort; after all, a considerable portion of the frame is formed by a leaf spring. There is no seat tube so the rider sits on the end of a spring. The rest of the frame is designed for torsional strength, which it achieves to a certain degree.

The seat can of course also be adjusted in height. Taller cyclists just pull the leaf spring a little further out of the frame, meaning that they have even softer suspension, whereas smaller, lighter people have a slightly harder, tighter suspension.

A manufacturer today would surely offer springs of differing hardness to cater to the varying weights of riders. The name Vélastic is even more ingenious than the bicycle itself, as it beautifully summarizes the machine's attributes in a single, evocative word.

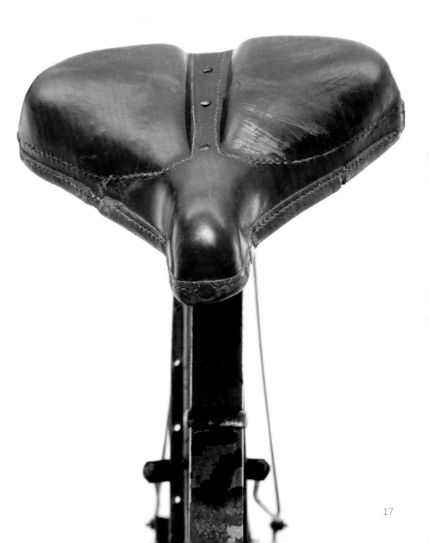

# CYCLES HIRONDELLE
## Rétro-Direct
## BACKWARDS AND FORWARDS

**VARIETY**
TOURING, CURIOSITY

**COUNTRY**
FRANCE

**DATE**
c. 1925

**WEIGHT**
18.7 KG (41.2 LB)

**FRAME**
VARNISHED STEEL, 55.8 CM (21.9 IN.) HIGH

**GEARS**
2

**BRAKES**
RIM SIDE PULL

**TYRES**
28 IN. WIRED

available. The Hirondelle reputation was excellent, after all, and the Rétro-Direct system, first introduced in 1903, had been on the market a long time already.

In 2007, an Englishman cycled the distance race Paris–Brest–Paris on an ancient Rétro-Direct, although over the 1,200-kilometre (746-mile) course the pedals dropped off several times – a small design blemish.

Incidentally, in the 1920s Hirondelle also created the first mass-produced front derailleur.

Anyone who wants a good transmission for cycling in the mountains but who absolutely refuses to change gear would find the Rétro-Direct by the Manufacture Française d'Armes et Cycles (or Hirondelle), a suitable alternative. As with every bicycle, it is possible to pedal forwards in flat terrain, but on a mountainside with the Rétro-Direct you move the cranks backwards.

What looks at first glance like a Möbius strip from the field of mechanical engineering is a refined redirecting mechanism for the chain. Two gears can be selected, but before those cyclists who think this is an easier ride get too excited, be aware that pedalling backwards uses different muscles. Riders can find themselves accessing muscles that are rarely used. This perhaps explains why the derailleur was favoured in the bicycle's evolution.

In the 1920s, however, the Rétro-Direct provided a serious alternative to the few gear systems then

# SCHULZ Funiculo
## COMFORT LEADS
## THE WAY

**VARIETY**
TOURING

**COUNTRY**
FRANCE

**DATE**
c. 1937

**WEIGHT**
14.8 KG (32.6 LB)

**FRAME**
VARNISHED STEEL, 53 CM (20.9 IN.) HIGH

**GEARS**
4, DERAILLEUR FUNICULO (REAR)

**BRAKES**
RIM SIDE PULL FUNICULO

**TYRES**
26 IN. WIRED

The extravagance of a Schulz Funiculo solo bike is obvious and is even more pronounced on the tandem.

The constructor Jacques Schulz was a master innovator, redesigning virtually every detail of his bicycles. The frame, which was created near Paris, was promoted from 1937 in cycling magazines as having *l'armature souple* – a flexible frame. The gear system on the Funiculo was able to cope with sprockets featuring up to 40 teeth, meaning that the bike climbed mountains easily with only one chain ring at the front. The front brake is an incredible example of thinking outside the box, and a very effective solution. The brakes were an unusual design with the rear brake activated through two cables running in parallel inside the frame, but the arms are not pivoted in the traditional sense – a marvel of technology. The cover in front of the seat tube, incidentally, is for stowing the bicycle pump.

For all the customized special effects, it might be surprising to note that the tyres are completely standard and can be damaged by simple glass splinters or nails. For such an extraordinary high-end bike, it is astonishing that humble road detritus can weaken it. Three Schulz bicycles are still known to exist in Europe; the Funiculo shown here is the only one that can still be ridden.

# HERCULES 2000 HK
## IN HIS FATHER'S FOOTSTEPS

**VARIETY**
URBAN

**COUNTRY**
GERMANY

**DATE**
c. 1958

**WEIGHT**
17.2 KG (37.9 LB)

**FRAME**
VARNISHED ALUMINIUM,
53.2 CM (20.9 IN.) HIGH

**GEARS**
3, HUB GEAR TORPEDO (REAR)

**BRAKES**
RIM SIDE PULL ALTENBURGER (FRONT),
COASTER BRAKE (REAR)

**TYRES**
26 IN. WIRED

If a bicycle in the late 1950s had the number 2000 in its name, then it probably aspired still to be ridden at the turn of the millennium. The sturdy Hercules 2000 HK had the traditional Hercules cross-frame, a distinctive feature of these bikes since 1889 – three years after the company was founded in Nuremberg, Germany.

The real innovation, though, was the frame material. It was cast from Silumin, an aluminium alloy, and the most advanced material of the time, and was the culmination of seven years of work. Originally designed by the engineer Hermann Klaue, the bicycle was launched at the Frankfurt bicycle exhibition in 1950. It created quite a sensation, but development did not pick up until the manufacturer Hercules took over construction in 1957. Soon afterwards, it was rolled out onto the market as the 'bike of the future'.

The 2000 HK model (the bicycle here is number 867099) was designed for men, women and children. The aluminium components were in perfect harmony with the frame, and a 3-speed Torpedo hub took care of speed and deceleration.

# MERVIL Mervilex
## SMALL BUT PERFECTLY FORMED

**VARIETY**
TOURING, CURIOSITY

**COUNTRY**
FRANCE

**DATE**
c. 1949

**WEIGHT**
17.5 KG (38.6 LB)

**FRAME**
VARNISHED STEEL, 55 CM (21.7 IN.) HIGH

**GEARS**
5, BRACKET GEAR (REAR)

**BRAKES**
RIM CENTRE PULL BERG LUX (FRONT), DRUM BRAKE
BESIDE BOTTOM BRACKET (REAR)

**TYRES**
26 IN. WIRED

In 1948 the B.U.E.C. (Boite Universelle d'Equipements pour Cycles) 'Vilex' gearshift system was the sensation of the cycling world – no other manufacturer before or since has offered five gears on the bottom bracket. The acronym translated as the 'universal gear system for equipping bicycles', which summed up the range and scope of its ambitions.

The Vilex invention was used by the marques Excell, Asterion and even Mervil. Indeed, Mervil and Vilex merged the two company names to form 'Mervilex', a beautifully poetic name for a new bicycle which perfectly conveyed the joy of riding. The newspaper advertisements depicted rather corpulent, cigar-smoking men flying up a mountain on their Mervilex or towing several trailers, one of which carried a voluptuous wife.

Mervil was based in Pontarlier in France, in the same neighbourhood as other bicycle brands such as Alcyon. It only existed from 1941 to 1950 and had a reputation for being innovative, possibly due to the fascinating Mervilex model alone.

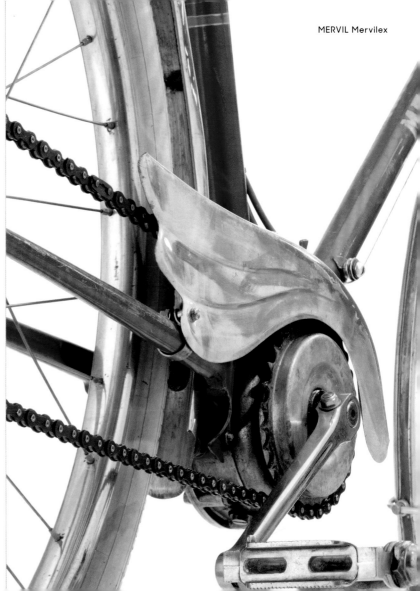

# GARIN
## BRAKING WITH HINGED HANDLEBARS

**VARIETY**
TOURING, CURIOSITY

**COUNTRY**
FRANCE

**DATE**
c. 1952

**WEIGHT**
16.6 KG (36.6 LB)

**FRAME**
VARNISHED STEEL, 55.5 CM (21.9 IN.) HIGH

**GEARS**
3, DERAILLEUR SUPER CHAMPION (REAR)

**BRAKES**
RIM SIDE PULL M.D.L. DEPOSE

**TYRES**
28 IN. WIRED (635)

In 1903 Maurice Garin won the very first Tour de France and, a year later, the second. He was subsequently stripped of his second medal for travelling some sections of the 1904 course by train and car to conserve energy. Garin was also a chain-smoker who often carried a bottle of red wine during bike races as a refreshing drink. Despite all this, he lived to the age of 86.

Garin used the boom years following World War II to establish his own bicycle company, along with a professional racing team. Garin's profile as a builder of bicycles was enhanced when Wim van Est of the Netherlands gained great success on one of his bicycles, and the Austrian Rudi Valenta excelled in the Bol d'Or in Paris in 1950.

In addition to racing bikes, Garin produced normal touring bikes, such as the example featured, which had no separate brake levers. To stop, the two ends of the hinged handlebars needed to be pushed together – although as this required using both hands, it meant that there was no opportunity to steer when braking.

# AFA
SUSPENSION,
BUT NOT AS
WE KNOW IT

**VARIETY**
TOURING, CURIOSITY

**COUNTRY**
FRANCE

**DATE**
1954

**WEIGHT**
13.2 KG (29.1 LB)

**FRAME**
VARNISHED STEEL, 56 CM (22 IN.) HIGH

**GEARS**
3, DERAILLEUR HURET TOURISTE LEGER (REAR)

**BRAKES**
RIM CENTRE PULL PYL

**TYRES**
26 IN. WIRED

In the early 1950s there were no smooth asphalt surfaces and few fine gravel cycle paths. The preoccupation, therefore, was how to create a comfortable ride, with suspension the key.

The French company AFA tested springs made from fibreglass rings supported by a stem with integrated suspension. As the saddle had no helpful springs and the downward tilting handlebars were rather crude, the most obvious shock absorber that this bicycle had was its rider.

It is the clarity of the general design, however, that is most noteworthy. Neat PYL brakes push the brake arm against the rim, and the sleek pedals have no axles.

# CHARREL
## THE SPEEDY
## ART OF TRAVEL

**VARIETY**
TOURING

**COUNTRY**
FRANCE

**DATE**
c. 1948

**WEIGHT**
12.7 KG (28 LB)

**FRAME**
VARNISHED STEEL, 60.7 CM (23.9 IN.) HIGH

**GEARS**
2 × 5, DERAILLEUR CYCLO (FRONT)
DERAILLEUR CHARREL (REAR)

**BRAKES**
RIM CENTRE PULL CHARREL

**TYRES**
26 IN. WIRED

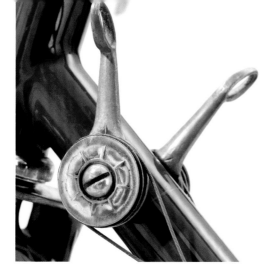

In quality terms, a Charrel touring bike was comparable to a Herse or Singer, but it lagged behind both in fame and numbers produced.

Paul Charrel was a passionate cyclist, and his exquisitely designed bicycles reflected his knowledge and love of the sport rather than his desire to be famous. He opened his business in 1936 in Lyon during a deep economic depression, and remained relatively unknown compared to his close neighbour, the famous constructor André Reiss.

The Charrel featured here (number 43) is a classic example: the tubes are all fillet-brazed (soldered) without using lugs (the highest discipline in frame building). Only the fork bears the beautiful spearpoint fork head. The Bowden cables run through the tubes, the rear stays are interwoven with the seat tube and top tube for added stability and the Cyclo gear is attached to a neat braze-on through four small tubes. In addition, the ingenious brakes, patented by Charrel in 1946, press the brake shoes against the rims, and the distance between the mudguards and the tyres can be finely adjusted by turning the stays. From modest beginnings come beautiful things.

# MERCIER
# MECADURAL
# Pélissier
## ULTRA-LIGHT DESIGN

**VARIETY**
TOURING

**COUNTRY**
FRANCE

**DATE**
c. 1950

**WEIGHT**
14.3 KG (31.5 LB)

**FRAME**
ALUMINIUM, 55.8 CM (22 IN.) HIGH

**GEARS**
2 × 3, DERAILLEUR SIMPLEX

**BRAKES**
RIM CENTRE PULL PYL

**TYRES**
26 IN. WIRED

The featherweight Pélissier featured here (number 32793) was a leader in lightening the load, with the only component heavier than necessary being its lights. The Pélissier belonged to the Mecadural series of aluminium bicycles, produced by Mercier after World War II.

In the thrifty years after the war, when steel use was being reserved for more essential products, aluminium became the lightweight, affordable and tough material of choice for bicycle frames, especially in France.

The mechanics of the Pélissier, however, may have compromised its integrity. With tubes anchored in the lugs through small expander components, this bicycle did not have the strength to last forever.

Other components survived better, such as the aluminium mudguards (with their unique wave design), the PYL brakes with the eccentric expansion cylinder-spreading mechanism and the bell that was moved by the front tyre (like a dynamo).

Francis Pélissier was the middle one of three brothers, all extremely successful in the cycling world. After a successful period as a professional cyclist he managed the La Perle team, whose rider, Hugo Koblet, won the Tour de France in 1951.

# RENÉ HERSE
## Diagonale
### THE CRÈME DE LA CRÈME OF TOURING BIKES

**VARIETY**
TOURING

**COUNTRY**
FRANCE

**DATE**
1969

**WEIGHT**
12.3 KG (27.2 LB)

**FRAME**
VARNISHED STEEL, 56.3 CM (22.1 IN.) HIGH

**GEARS**
2 × 5, DERAILLEUR HURET LUXE

**BRAKES**
RIM CENTRE PULL WEINMANN 610 VAINQUEUR 999

**TYRES**
28 IN. WIRED

René Herse ran a speciality bicycle shop in the Parisian suburb of Levallois. It was not far from Alex Singer, the famous artisan bicycle manufacturer and adopted patron saint of French frame makers.

Every original Herse frame was an artwork with practically every component a braze-on (soldered). The quality of parts and skilled labour used to build a Herse bicycle were the best possible, reflected in the astronomical retail price (about three to four months' average wages). For Herse lovers, however, no price was too high.

The name of the René Herse Diagonale suggested the bicycle's real purpose – as the perfect touring vehicle for 'Les Diagonales'. A popular activity for many decades of cyclists, racing between the six cities on the rough diagonals of France was a long-distance challenge.

The René Herse frame shown here is number 6955.

# RENÉ HERSE
## Demontable
## FIRST OF THE
## FOLDING BICYCLES

**VARIETY**
FOLDING, TOURING

**COUNTRY**
FRANCE

**DATE**
1968

**WEIGHT**
11 KG (24.3 LB)

**FRAME**
VARNISHED STEEL, 58.9 CM (23.2 IN.) HIGH

**GEARS**
2 × 5, DERAILLEUR HURET LUXE

**BRAKES**
RIM CENTRE PULL WEINMANN 610 VAINQUEUR 999

**TYRES**
28 IN. WIRED

Herse bicycles are admired for their perfection and lovingly crafted details. The Demontable model featured here (number 6861) was no different. It aimed to be a luxury bicycle that could be taken apart and was, therefore, infinitely mobile.

Displayed flatpacked in the boot of a car at the Paris cycling exhibition in the early 1960s, the Demontable was one of the first generation of folding bicycles. Its reputation grew massively through its championing by a doctor, Clifford Graves, in the USA. Through this transatlantic promotion, the Demontable made it out of the Levallois suburbs in Paris, and into the world. With Americans packing the neat Demontable to take travelling, they were able, ironically, to see Europe from the seat of their own bike.

The Bike Friday – New World Tourist (page 206) followed on from this idea nearly 30 years later.

# WINORA
## Take-Off
### FROM BIG
### TO SMALL

**VARIETY**
FOLDING

**COUNTRY**
GERMANY

**DATE**
1989

**WEIGHT**
11.1 KG (24.5 LB)

**FRAME**
VARNISHED STEEL, 57 CM (22.4 IN.) HIGH

**GEARS**
2 × 6, DERAILLEUR SACHS ARIS NEW SUCCESS

**BRAKES**
RIM SIDE PULL MODOLO

**TYRES**
28 IN. WIRED

Once German reunification occurred in 1990, the Winora company in Schweinfurt, Bavaria was exposed to new markets. With an aggressive sales strategy and a keen eye on the competition, it quickly developed new bicycle designs.

The Winora Take-off road bike, designed by Ernst Brust, could be folded up and carried in a special case. The handlebars, front wheel and saddle could be dismantled using quick-release skewers. Pedals could then be taken off with a bayonet fitting, and the rear wheel detached through removing the wheel spindle, leaving the sprockets and chain attached to the frame and the rider with clean fingers. The seat stays then needed to be split using a quick fastener, and the rear part of the frame folded forwards. The Take-off could then fit in its case.

The Winora Take-off featured opposite (number 91) weighs just over 11 kilograms. The Sachs-Huret New Success ARIS (Advanced Rider Index System) components were progressive technology in 1988. A proper slant parallelogram design with two sprung pivots gave the bicycle a smart individual look, notable for its angular styling and the placing of the adjustment screws. It proved a reasonably successful design, although it did not match Shimano's level of attention to chains and freewheel cogs. The example shown here is the short pulley cage version.

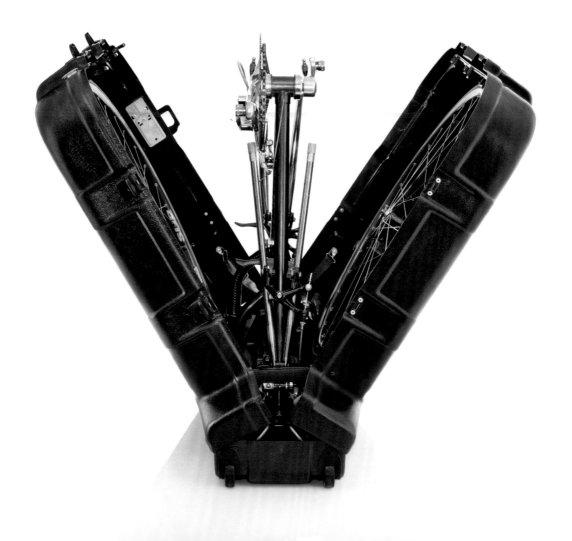

# BRIDGESTONE
## Grandtech
## ON THEIR
## OWN TYRES

VARIETY
FOLDING

COUNTRY
JAPAN

DATE
1986

WEIGHT
13.3 KG (29.3 LB)

FRAME
VARNISHED STEEL, 54.2 CM (21.3 IN.) HIGH

GEARS
6, DERAILLEUR SUNTOUR (REAR)

BRAKES
RIM SIDE PULL DIA COMPE

TYRES
28 IN. WIRED

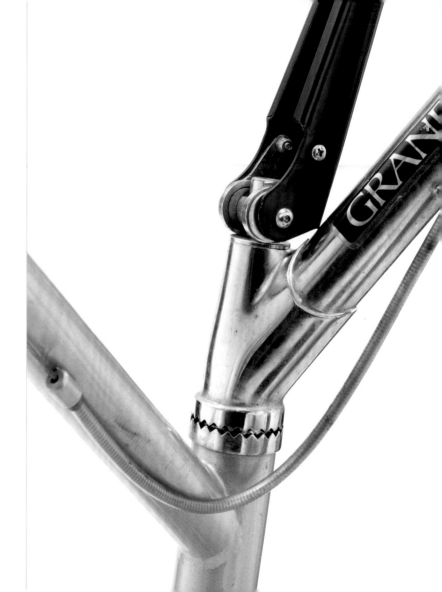

Bridgestone is best known as a manufacturer of tyres, and the brand's bicycles (along with their motorbikes, which were produced between 1960 and 1971) lie in their shadow. Undeservedly so, at least when some light is cast on the most dazzling part of the history of Bridgestone bicycles.

Grant Petersen led the American branch of Bridgestone with visionary and single-minded ambition. Consistently ignoring all the fast-moving trends, he favoured innovative, intelligent solutions, compact parts and Japanese precision and reliability. Petersen worked all these components into on-road and off-road bicycles. His bicycles were clever and unique, and came at an affordable price.

The Bridgestone Grandtech, for example, was an immensely elegant folding bike. Its handlebars and pedals folded away and the frame bent in the middle, yet it still rode like a light women's sport bike.

After Bridgestone discontinued operations in the USA in 1994, Petersen continued his work with his own company, Rivendell – extremely successful to this day. Bridgestone is also still making bicycles from its own factory in Japan. Some of the frames manufactured there have received the much sought-after JKA (Japanese Keirin Association) approval – and so can be ridden in the Keirin sprint races that originated in Japan.

Bridgestone, incidentally, also collaborated with vehicle designer Alex Moulton, and the tyres and the modern Moulton F-frame came from Japan.

# DIAMANT
## Handy Bike
HANDLING A
HEAVY WEIGHT

**VARIETY**
FOLDING, CURIOSITY

**COUNTRY**
GERMANY

**DATE**
1993

**WEIGHT**
15.1 KG (33.3 LB)

**FRAME**
STAINLESS STEEL, 54 CM (21.3 IN.) HIGH

**GEARS**
7, HUB GEAR SHIMANO (REAR)

**BRAKES**
RIM CENTRE PULL SHIMANO ALTUS (FRONT),
COASTER BRAKE (REAR)

**TYRES**
26 IN. WIRED

The benefits of a stainless-steel frame is that it will not rust, does not scratch (when the bike is folded carelessly) and never has to be painted. The frame on the Diamant Handy Bike is fiendishly heavy, however, which matters particularly because it is a folding bike.

The epithet 'Handy' hints at a small and light bike, but with a weight of 15.1 kilograms (33.3 lb) its name turns out to be a hollow promise. After a catch on the bottom bracket is released, the front part of the Diamant folds backwards. In order to carry this bike away, you would need to be as strong as an ox.

Even riding away is not all that straightforward either. A label on the frame advises that it is 'not suitable for publicly accessible areas (road traffic, country lanes, forest tracks and meadow paths)'.

The frame was patented in 1991 by John S. Strozyk, an American living in Hanover, and called the 'Intraframe Folding Bicycle'. The Diamant Handy Bike is clearly based on this patent, and was showcased in 1993 at the IFMA (Internationale Fahrrad- und Motorrad-Ausstellung) in Cologne, an international bicycle and motorbike exhibition. Later that year it went on sale for 1,500 DM (about double the cost of a standard folding bike).

# BMW
# Super-Tech
## A NAME FOR THE
## TERRAIN

**VARIETY**
FOLDING, MOUNTAIN, RACING

**COUNTRY**
GERMANY

**DATE**
1997

**WEIGHT**
13.3 KG (29.3 LB)

**FRAME**
ALUMINIUM, VARNISHED STEEL,
48.3 CM (19 IN.) HIGH

**GEARS**
3 × 9, DERAILLEUR SHIMANO XTR

**BRAKES**
RIM V-BRAKE SHIMANO XTR

**TYRES**
26 IN. WIRED

The features of the BMW Super-Tech mountain bike borrowed heavily from the car and motorbikes for which the German manufacturer is famous. (See also the Subaru 2WD Dual Power, page 54.)

The telelever system (developed by HS Products and adopted by BMW) provided an anti-dive effect, so that the bike barely dipped forward at all when braking. As a result, the risk of the rider going over the handlebars was drastically reduced. On the other hand, the response was not as sensitive as with the best suspension forks.

The Super-Tech was truly revolutionary, however. It was a full-suspension folding bike, which made the journey to forests and mountains significantly easier for those wishing to drive there.

When purchasing the bike, customers also received detachable mudguards, lights, an air pump for the suspension elements, a good user manual and a repair manual.

The brand may be German, but the aluminium frames for this line were produced in Bologna, Italy.

The model featured here is number 038322.

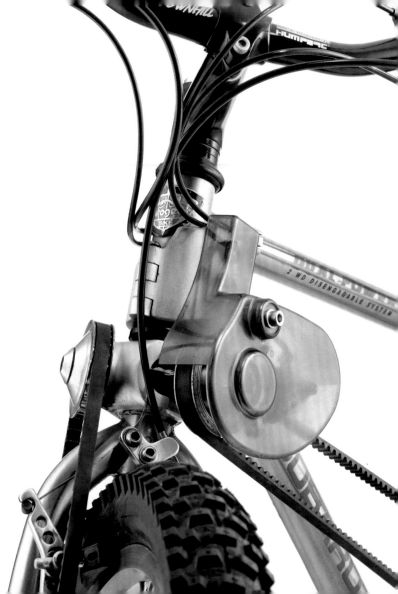

# SUBARU
## 2WD Dual Power
## AN ALL-WHEEL DRIVE

**VARIETY**
MOUNTAIN, CURIOSITY

**COUNTRY**
AUSTRIA / TAIWAN

**DATE**
1996

**WEIGHT**
15.4 KG (34 LB)

**FRAME**
CLEAR-COATED STEEL, 48.2 CM (19 IN.) HIGH

**GEARS**
3 × 7, DERAILLEUR SHIMANO STX

**BRAKES**
RIM CANTILEVER DIA COMPE

**TYRES**
26 IN. WIRED

Any component that supplies perfect traction to a car could also be applied to a bike – so thought Günter Kappacher when he set about assembling mountain bikes in the late 1980s. He worked for a furniture company, along with running a bicycle repair shop, and over the years the ideas of this handyman took shape.

Kappacher created an all-wheel drive to be used for bicycles, and in 1993 the car-tuning company Oettinger made the idea a reality. The sculptor and racing cyclist Paul Pollanka then paved the way for series production. His knack for technical tinkering solved the last few problems, and simultaneously initiated the process of serial manufacture in Taiwan.

The front wheel was driven by a connectable toothed belt. This all-wheel drive technology was patented, and the name Progear appeared on the bikes. Other bikes were added to the programme, but in the time it took to move the development on, virtually every mountain bike on the market had been fitted with a suspension fork. The full-suspension prototype conceived by Paul Pollanka with Horst Leitner's AMP fork was put on hold.

Years passed until in the mid-1990s a few car manufacturers grew interested in widening their market and producing bicycle spin-offs (see the BMW Super-Tech on page 52). There could have been no better partner for Subaru than the Progear, and in 1996–97 around 180 all-wheel drive mountain bikes were sold to Subaru Germany. The bicycle featured is number ZW30014, and it rides just as exquisitely as the team of inventors promised.

# BREEZER
## Beamer
### A DIFFERENT KIND OF SUSPENSION

**VARIETY**
MOUNTAIN

**COUNTRY**
USA

**DATE**
c. 1992

**WEIGHT**
11.6 KG (25.6 LB)

**FRAME**
VARNISHED STEEL/CARBON,
ADJUSTABLE HEIGHT

**GEARS**
3 × 7, DERAILLEUR SHIMANO
DEORE XT

**BRAKES**
RIM CANTILEVER SHIMANO XTR

**TYRES**
26 IN. WIRED

Mike and Jim Allsop presented the first bike with a springy saddle post at the Interbike International Trade Expo in California in 1989. They called it Softride Suspension Systems, and this unusual idea, although not completely original (see the Vialle Vélastic on page 16), was promptly awarded the first prize.

In 1991 the first mountain bike based on this idea was conceived.

Mountain bike legend Joe Breeze was already involved and, in addition to a viscoelastic spring element for the saddle post, he attempted to smooth the path for this mountain bike through front suspension. The suspension, known as Softride, proved a success. The Beamer was the first mountain bike with complete suspension to win the Downhill World Championships in 1992.

The frame below the transverse spring elements consisted of steel, and the winning bike had steel springs in the fork and rear. It was later found that this construction was more suitable for road-racing bikes. The number of the model featured is H30020214, and new models of the Breezer Beamer are still manufactured today.

# C-4
## LESS IS MORE

**VARIETY**
MOUNTAIN

**COUNTRY**
ITALY

**DATE**
c. 1988

**WEIGHT**
10.5 KG (23.1 LB)

**FRAME**
VARNISHED CARBON, 54 CM (21.2 IN.) HIGH

**GEARS**
3 × 8, DERAILLEUR SHIMANO DEORE

**BRAKES**
RIM CANTILEVER SHIMANO XT

**TYRES**
26 IN. WIRED

The C-4 bicycle reduced its weight by omitting a tube; it also provided suspension in this manner. The idea had origins almost one hundred years previously, when the Coventry Machinists' Company, UK, had experimented with frames without a seat tube on their 'Swift' safety bike. The C-4 adopted the concept in 1985, and the manufacturer Colnago took up the idea in 1989 for their mountain bike C35. The material used in the frame of the C-4 was exclusively forward-looking, however, with the carbon monocoque created using an NJC (No Joint Construction) method. The frame provided effective shock-absorption through the fork, and additional front suspension was used on the stem.

# SCHAUFF
## Wall Street
### BUSINESS AS UNUSUAL

**VARIETY**
URBAN

**COUNTRY**
GERMANY

**DATE**
1993

**WEIGHT**
11.6 KG (25.6 LB)

**FRAME**
VARNISHED CARBON, 50 CM (19.7 IN.) HIGH

**GEARS**
3 × 8, DERAILLEUR SHIMANO XTR

**BRAKES**
RIM CANTILEVER SHIMANO XTR

**TYRES**
28 IN. WIRED

60

The modern design of the Schauff Wall Street jars with the vintage of its long-established creator. The Schauff bicycle factory was founded by Hans and Barbara Schauff for the manufacture of racing bike frames in 1932 in Cologne – within spitting distance of the Six Day Races. When war damage forced them to move premises, Schauff continued to build in Remagen am Rhein, Germany.

In 1991 Schauff commenced work on the development of their bow design, and the 'blow moulding method' was used to produce perfect carbon fibre-reinforced plastic frames. In 1992 the Schauff Wall Street was awarded the 'Rote Punkt' design prize, which later became the coveted benchmark known as the 'red dot design award'.

The Wall Street is a trekking bike disguised as a mountain bike with, ironically, narrow 700C tyres borrowed from a racing bike. The exquisite detail and internal cables tell of a passion for precision, but although the stem may take care of the suspension, the saddle does look a little painful. Only around 20 copies of this model were produced.

# SLINGSHOT
## WITH CABLE AND SPRING

**VARIETY**
FOLDING, CURIOSITY

**COUNTRY**
USA

**DATE**
c. 1991

**WEIGHT**
11.9 KG (26.3 LB)

**FRAME**
VARNISHED STEEL, 47 CM (18.5 IN.) HIGH

**GEARS**
3 × 7, DERAILLEUR SHIMANO XTR

**BRAKES**
RIM CANTILEVER SHIMANO XTR

**TYRES**
26 IN. WIRED

The Slingshot design is the result of an accident in 1985, when Mark Groendal from Grand Rapids, Michigan, broke the down tube on his mini motorbike. The surprising result was a more comfortable ride, although this was not sustainable in the long run, so a more permanent solution had to be found.

For his first attempts at designing a bicycle without suspension forks or a sprung rear frame section, Groendal continued playing with this idea, using an old ski for the top tube. Later variations included three steel top tubes and two cables in place of the down tube. He finally arrived at the best design: one top tube attached to a fibreglass bridge and one steel cable with a spring. The level of comfort is determined by the pre-stressing and, so can be adjusted. The frame components, which look normal from the outside, are also reinforced internally in some sections – to avoid buckling in the same way that Groendal's mini motorbike once did.

# CANNONDALE
# F2000
## URBAN SLEEK

**VARIETY**
URBAN

**COUNTRY**
USA

**DATE**
c. 2002

**WEIGHT**
10.1 KG (22.3 LB)

**FRAME**
VARNISHED ALUMINIUM,
51.9 CM (24.4 IN.) HIGH

**GEARS**
3 × 9, DERAILLEUR SHIMANO XTR

**BRAKES**
DISC BRAKE MAGURA MARTA

**TYRES**
28 IN. WIRED

For anyone who preferred to take an original Cannondale mountain bike out on flatter terrain, the 'urban poser' look was quickly achieved through fitting slimline 700C tyres. The manufacturer went on to produce a number of roadworthy models, including the 'Lefty', that have enriched the cycling world for over a decade.

The Cannondale F2000 boasts only half a fork. It is lightweight, owing to the perfect balance of materials and structural detail. The components used for head tube suspension in head-shock systems are moved to the other half of the fork, reducing the unsprung mass. The CAAD (Cannondale Advanced Aluminium Design) 5-model frame is hand-welded from 6061–T6 aluminium, a metal with good mechanical properties and weldability. The frame is then heat-treated to guarantee optimum hardness and strength.

# BIOMEGA MN01
## STAND OUT FROM THE CROWD

**VARIETY**
URBAN

**COUNTRY**
DENMARK

**DATE**
c. 2001

**WEIGHT**
11.9 KG (26.2 LB)

**FRAME**
VARNISHED ALUMINIUM,
44.5 CM (17.5 IN.) HIGH

**GEARS**
14, HUB GEAR ROHLOFF SPEEDHUB (REAR)

**BRAKES**
DISC BRAKE MAGURA MARTA

**TYRES**
26 IN. WIRED

The Biomega MN01 is the ultimate designer bicycle – it boasts a profile resembling a sprinter on the starting blocks. Founders Jens Martin Skibsted and Elias Grove Nielsen sought to create a dynamic and unconventional bicycle, and to this end they approached an unorthodox collaborator – product designer Marc Newson.

Skibsted's sketches for a high-end city bicycle combined with Newson's vision to produce a distinctive design. The Biomega MN01 has an unusual superplastic aluminium frame formed from two semi-monocoques (a by-product of this is the noisy ride as the frame acts as amplifier). The Rohloff speed hubs also depart from traditional ways of thinking with 14 integrated gears that require no maintenance and have the ability to change gear under load. They are, on the other hand, as expensive and heavy as a mid-range mountain bicycle, confirming the MN01 as a designer product in both attitude and price tag.

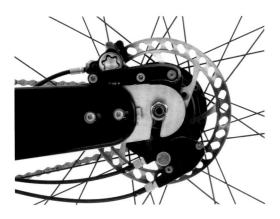

# BIRIA Unplugged
# TM-Design
## CRAFTSMANSHIP
## HAS ITS PRICE

**VARIETY**
URBAN, CURIOSITY

**COUNTRY**
GERMANY

**DATE**
c. 1998

**WEIGHT**
12.2 KG (26.9 LB)

**FRAME**
CLEAR-COATED CARBON,
50 CM (19.7 IN.) HIGH

**GEARS**
3 × 8, DERAILLEUR SACHS QUARZ

**BRAKES**
DISC BRAKE
SACHS POWER DISC

**TYRES**
26 IN. WIRED

You could find beauty in the mud with the designer Biria Unplugged TM-Design mountain bike. Despite it having a body to marvel at, however, its performance was less attractive.

Everything here was made of carbon and constructed at mind-boggling expense. The wheels, for example, were only attached on one hub side, but because of the shape of the frame and the spokes, pedalling forces were perfectly aligned. Suspension, and the prohibitive cost of production, were overlooked, and around 27 bicycles were created. Of these, more than half were assembled to make complete bikes, with the rest auctioned off unbuilt.

An obstacle to success was a price tag that ranged from 14,000 to 22,000 DM (£4,800 to £7,500), at a time when other high-end mountain bikes cost between 3,000 and 7,000 DM (£1000 to £2400). Even the 24-carat hard gold plating on the chain of the top model made no difference (and could only partially hide the fact that the frame is particularly weak when riding out of the saddle).

# LOTUS Sport 110
## THE ULTIMATE
## RECORD BREAKER

**VARIETY**
RACING

**COUNTRY**
UNITED KINGDOM

**DATE**
1994

**WEIGHT**
9.9 KG (21.8 LB)

**FRAME**
CLEAR-COATED CARBON,
ADJUSTABLE HEIGHT

**GEARS**
2 × 8, DERAILLEUR SHIMANO
DURA-ACE

**BRAKES**
RIM SIDE PULL SHIMANO DURA-ACE

**TYRES**
27 IN. TUBULAR

When the International Cycling Union (UCI) relaxed its strict regulations governing bicycle frames in the early 1990s, designer Mike Burrows and the technicians at Lotus grasped the moment. Reversioning a monocoque frame that Burrows had been working on since the mid-1980s, they also used carbon composite to make the frame incredibly lightweight.

The resulting superbike, the Lotus Sport 110, was revolutionary. It quickly made cycling history with Britain's Chris Boardman racing it to gold-medal victory at the 1992 Olympic Games, and shortly afterwards taking the 5,000- metre world record.

Lotus racing models were followed by the 'street' version, shown here. This was more affordable – at only the price of a small car.

# CINETICA Giotto
## A COLLECTOR'S TREASURE TROVE

**VARIETY**
RACING

**COUNTRY**
ITALY

**DATE**
1990

**WEIGHT**
9.8 KG (21.6 LB)

**FRAME**
VARNISHED CARBON, 57.6 CM (22.7 IN.) HIGH

**GEARS**
2 × 8, DERAILLEUR CAMPAGNOLO

**BRAKES**
RIM CENTRE PULL CAMPAGNOLO C RECORD DELTA

**TYRES**
27 IN. TUBULAR

74

The carbon monocoque frame of the Cinetica Giotto appeared to be lightweight, but being manufactured as they were, they were anything but. With the first prototypes made from two semi-monocoques bonded together, the single monocoque frame was eventually achieved and was able to show off its talents.

The Giotto frame was about 500 grammes (1.2 lb) lighter than the best steel frame of the time, and its impressive torsional strength outclassed every lightweight construction concept of the late 1980s. Only the bottom bracket twisted (imperceptibly to the rider) around the longitudinal axis. The suspension was a particular treat, as the missing seat tube gave an incredibly comfortable ride.

The creator of the Cinetica Giotto was Andrea Cinelli, son of the legendary Cino Cinelli (see the Cinelli Laser on page 250), together with scientists from the University of Milan. It even boasted unique features such as a computer timer integrated with the saddle to give prescient racing data. With initial promising plans for high-end series production, the Giotto looked as if it had a bright future ahead of it. It was brought down in the end, however, by the most mundane of problems: the moulds for producing the frames broke, leaving only about 50 finished frames. These completed Giottos are now coveted collectors' items, with only a handful still known; the model featured opposite is number 1010.

# KESTREL 200 SCi
## SHIFTING WITH ELECTRICITY

**VARIETY**
RACING

**COUNTRY**
USA

**DATE**
c. 1993

**WEIGHT**
9.7 KG (21.4 LB)

**FRAME**
VARNISHED CARBON,
56 CM (22 IN.) HIGH

**GEARS**
2 × 8 DERAILLEUR
MAVIC ZAP

**BRAKES**
RIM SIDE PULL MAVIC

**TYRES**
27 IN. TUBULAR

'This is the design that changed the direction of modern cycling,' wrote one American in a report on the Kestrel. It was a bike that was looking to the future. Along with other exciting new developments in bicycle construction, such as carbon monocoques – see the Bianchi C-4 (page 256), Cinetica Giotto (page 74) and Lotus Sport 110 (page 72) – and the slow modernizing of traditional construction techniques – for example, the aluminium lugs of the Colnago Carbitubo Pista (page 84) – the Kestrel's design marked it out as part of the new crowd.

It had Zap Mavic System electrically controlled gear shifters, which were the first micro-processor driven rear dérailleur. The ZAP had been tested at the Tour de France by the ONCE and RMO teams.

An advanced idea, the use of electronics was ambitious. Although the theory was simply to press a button to shift the gears, in practice it was not that straightforward. Even the wireless Mektronic, the successor version that appeared in 1999, was not without problems.

Only now are electronic shifters gradually being rediscovered, this time by manufacturers such as Campagnolo and Shimano. The model featured here is number 59003.

# INBIKE / TEXTIMA
## FROM EAST
## TO WEST

**VARIETY**
RACING, SINGLESPEED

**COUNTRY**
GERMANY/
EAST GERMANY

**DATE**
c. 1990

**WEIGHT**
8.7 KG (19.2 LB)

**FRAME**
VARNISHED STEEL,
56.8 CM (22.4 IN.) HIGH

**GEAR**
1, FIXED

**TYRES**
27 IN. TUBULAR

The roots of this time trial bike go back to East Germany, but it was not built until after German reunification. A specialist department of the Textima company (which built textile machines as a day-to-day business) also produced racing bikes for elite cyclists. The precision and quality of their construction caused a furore in international competitions.

After reunification, the Textima legacy was carefully managed by Christoph Hähle and carried on under the name of Inbike. The reinforcement plates were typical of later Textima bikes. The carbon handlebars by the Italian firm 3ttt, developed by Paolo Martin, head designer for Pininfarina, were a perfect match. In the second half of the 1980s these handlebars could be found almost universally on time trial bikes.

The Dura-Ace-10 parts, with their subtle reduction in size, are also noteworthy. Instead of half an inch (12.7 mm), the chain pitch measures 10 millimetres, which makes the chain ring, for instance, smaller, by 21 per cent. It is also lighter by 38 per cent – mass that does not need to be accelerated when sprinting. However, bicycle evolution decided to neglect this invention, perhaps because changing the chain norms was considered too complex.

The number of the model featured is 112062.

# SCHAUFF Aero
## HANDLEBARS FROM THE WIND TUNNEL

**VARIETY**
RACING, SINGLESPEED

**COUNTRY**
WEST GERMANY

**DATE**
1980

**WEIGHT**
7.7 KG (17 LB)

**FRAME**
VARNISHED STEEL,
46.5 CM (18.3 IN.) HIGH

**GEAR**
1, FIXED

**TYRES**
27 IN. TUBULAR

Aerodynamics was a competitive field in the late 1970s and early 1980s, with the reputation of entire nations and ideologies at stake in the race for victory.

Testing in wind tunnels was common, and Schauff used tunnels belonging to Mercedes-Benz, the car manufacturer, to develop a track bike designed purely for speed.

The appropriately named Schauff Aero (the featured model is number 555) had handlebars that were integrated into the fork. It was not an original idea as Assos had showcased a similar fork/handlebar design on a track bike as early as 1978, and other designs were known in the German Democratic Republic, Soviet Union and USA.

Despite this, Schauff bikes were an attractive option for the professional cyclist, and were ridden by Freddy Schmidke (runner-up on the time trial track in 1982) and Petra Stegherr, the 1984 German national champion. Stegherr claimed seventh place in the World Championships in the same year and took fourteenth place in the women's Tour de France in 1985.

# PEKA Peka
## LEANING
## FORWARDS

**VARIETY**
RACING, SINGLESPEED

**COUNTRY**
NETHERLANDS

**DATE**
c. 1985

**WEIGHT**
11 KG (24.3 LB)

**FRAME**
VARNISHED STEEL,
59.1 CM (23.3 IN.) HIGH

**GEAR**
1, FIXED

**TYRES**
24 IN. TUBULAR (FRONT),
27 IN. TUBULAR (REAR)

The World motor-paced Championships were staged for the last time in 1994. Their demise seems surprising, given the enthusiasm that led to this becoming the most popular form of cycling in the early 20th century. Today motor-paced – or 'stayer' – races have been mainly forgotten.

The bikes that excelled in stayer races were developed specifically to sit in the slipstream created by the heavy motorcycle in front. This meant a Peka bicycle (made by Peter Serier of the Peperkamp bicycle shop in Amsterdam) could reach speeds of up to 100 kilometres (44.7 miles) per hour. The ambitious Peka worked beautifully, and the 66-tooth front chain ring also helps explain the high top velocity. It is impossible to start the bicycle because of its high gearing, so help is needed. Once under way, the stayer must never leave the pacer's slipstream and because of the 24-inch front wheel and the back curved fork, the stayer can get very close to the pacer (the fork also provides better stability). If the stayer does get too close, a rear-mounted roller on the motorcycle prevents a fall.

The stability of the bike though was easily affected if a draught from a passing motorcycle caught the front disc wheel (at this time an expensive and ambitious innovation). Sadly such dangerous turbulence could only be avoided by returning to a more standard spoked wheel.

It goes without saying that riding in the slipstream of a motorbike meant inhaling exhaust fumes, although this was not always the case in stayer races. In the past, stayers rode behind bicycles with several seats and, later, behind tandem electric motorbikes.

The featured model is number 0222E38BDR59.

# COLNAGO
## Carbitubo Pista
### THE EARLY
### CARBON ERA

**VARIETY**
RACING, SINGLESPEED

**COUNTRY**
ITALY

**DATE**
c. 1990

**WEIGHT**
8.2 KG (18.1 LB)

**FRAME**
CLEAR-COATED CARBON/
ALUMINIUM LUGS, 56.7 CM
(22.3 IN.) HIGH

**GEAR**
1, FIXED

**TYRES**
26 IN. TUBULAR (FRONT),
27 IN. TUBULAR (REAR)

In the early years of using carbon as a frame material, it was known for being expensive and not necessarily simple to work with.

The monocoque frame still belonged to a distant world in 1975, when the first carbon frame (mixed with aluminium) was built in the USA. However, Colnago ventured forward with its own ideas of a carbon future. The Colnago Carbitubo Pista model was presented at the 1988 IFMA (Internationale Fahrrad- und Motorrad-Ausstellung). Its carbon tubes came from Ferrari, a worthy supplier for a bike whose sole requirement is speed. Its carbon tubes were bonded to one another using aluminium lugs and they could, as you may suspect, become detached at the bond when under stress. From a purely aesthetic point of view, however, the two slender down tubes are beautiful. Fewer than 20 machines were produced.

Structurally, the aluminium lugs of the Carbitubo Pista were virtually identical to those used by the well-known manufacturer Alan, which was also producing frames made from carbon tubes and aluminium lugs.

To this day Colnago is probably the most famous bicycle brand, and a book listing all the victories won on Colnago bikes would run to several volumes.

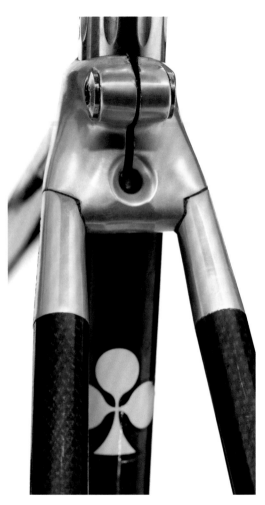

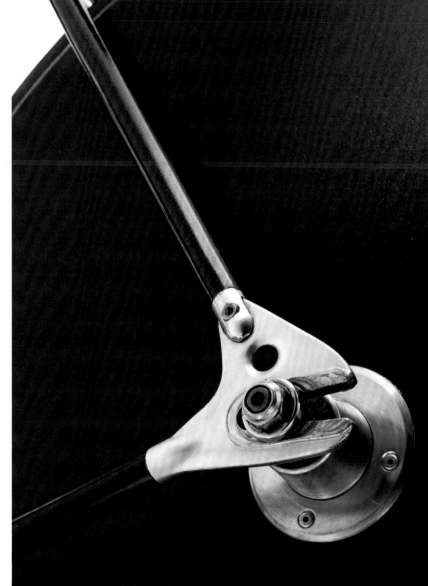

# SABLIÈRE
## A CURVACEOUS BEAUTY

**VARIETY**
RACING

**COUNTRY**
FRANCE

**DATE**
c. 1978

**WEIGHT**
8.5 KG (18.7 LB)

**FRAME**
POLISHED ALUMINIUM,
59 CM (23.2 IN.) HIGH

**GEARS**
2 × 7, DERAILLEUR
MAVIC 862 (FRONT),
DERAILLEUR MAVIC 851 (BACK)

**BRAKES**
RIM CENTRE PULL
CAMPAGNOLO C. RECORD DELTA

**TYRES**
27 IN. TUBULAR

The Sablière's unpainted aluminium frame boasts sleek, flowing tubes with perfectly filed and polished welds. The sensuous curves of the handlebars provide the finishing touches to this attractive bike and are reminiscent of high-spec aeroplane design.

With time-trial machines such as this, the race is against the clock rather than the opposition. All that can potentially harm the Sablière's clean line is a side wind across the back wheel. To counteract this, and retain good stability while riding, there are centrifugal weights in the back wheel; as the wheel rotates faster the weights move outwards, assuring an unwavering course.

Since the 1930s aluminium frames have been made in France by Nicola Barra and Pierre Colin. It is only in recent years, however, that aluminium has made a breakthrough into the international market as a widely used frame material.

# MECACYCLE
## Turbo Bonanza
## NOT JUST SPLIT SEAT TUBES

**VARIETY**
RACING, CURIOSITY

**COUNTRY**
FRANCE

**DATE**
c. 1985

**WEIGHT**
11 KG (24.3 LB)

**FRAME**
VARNISHED STEEL,
58 CM (22.8 IN.) HIGH

**GEARS**
2 × 7, DERAILLEUR HURET

**BRAKES**
RIM CENTRE PULL WEINMANN DELTA

**TYRES**
26 IN. TUBULAR (FRONT),
27 IN. TUBULAR (REAR)

Raymond Creuset was known for his creativity even before establishing Mecacycle. He had worked as a trained mechanic for Mercier, then for a think tank specializing in solving complex technical problems before moving into the bicycle business at the beginning of the 1980s. Creuset bought Mecacycle, a rather unsuccessful bike factory in St Etienne, the cycling capital of France, and the company quickly caused a sensation with its new design. The 'turbo' frame featured the split seat tube (see also the Rigi Bici Corta on page 174) and became the focus of public interest at the 1982 IFMA in Cologne.

The Bonanza was just such a Mecacycle 'turbo'. It was named after a Swiss bicycle dealer who sold Mecacycle frames and supplied a particular team of professionals.

The handling was perfect and well balanced, even though the wheelbase was kept short due to the split seat tube and a 26-inch front wheel.

# DIAMANT
## Ironman SLX
BEST FOOT FORWARDS

**VARIETY**
RACING, CURIOSITY

**COUNTRY**
BELGIUM

**DATE**
1992

**WEIGHT**
10.2 KG (22.5 LB)

**FRAME**
VARNISHED STEEL,
56.5 CM (22.2 IN.) HIGH

**GEARS**
2 × 8, DERAILLEUR
SHIMANO DURA-ACE

**BRAKES**
RIM SIDE PULL
SHIMANO DURA-ACE

**TYRES**
28 IN. WIRED

Diamant is a name with plenty of charisma, and several bicycle companies have adopted it for a model. The manufacturer of the Diamant Ironman SLX has its home in Belgium, where a keen delight in design is encouraged.

Launched in the early 1990s, this particularly forward-leaning model was designed for extreme triathletes and looked as if it was constantly riding with a tail wind. Thanks to its special geometry, the Diamant Ironman SLX does not need the seatpost bent forwards. Anyone unfamiliar with the sport of cycling could be forgiven for thinking it is a caricature of a triathlon bike, with its typically steep frame-angles and distinctive seatposts and handlebars. The Ironman seems to distort these features to an almost grotesque effect.

It is possible, however, that the designer took inspiration from a 1940s cartoon showing a similar bicycle in the Tour de France. The cartoonist's bicycle may be exaggerated for effect, but it looks similar to this high-performance and very serious machine.

# BOB JACKSON
## Super Legend
### HETCHINS' LONG ARM

**VARIETY**
RACING, TOURING

**COUNTRY**
UNITED KINGDOM

**DATE**
2002

**WEIGHT**
11 KG (24.3 LB)

**FRAME**
VARNISHED / CHROMED STEEL,
59.8 CM (23.5 IN.) HIGH

**GEARS**
3 × 9, DERAILLEUR
SHIMANO ULTEGRA

**BRAKES**
RIM SIDE PULL
SHIMANO ULTEGRA

**TYRES**
28 IN. WIRED

The Bob Jackson company is older than its name. In 1935, it produced bicycles as J. R. J. Cycles and continued to do so under the name Merlin. Only in 1961 did the company become famous under its present name. The particularly high-end special-edition models bore the name Bob Jackson, after the new owner of J. R. J. Cycles, and that hasn't changed to this day. In 1969 the company also started selling under this name in the USA.

At the end of the 1970s Bob Jackson was commissioned to make the famous Hetchins frame with the 'curly stays' (the curved rear stays) and the elaborately filed lugs. In 1986, the Bob Jackson company and Hetchins merged.

The Bob Jackson Super Legend has the lugs of the Hetchins' top model, the Magnum Opus (the benchmark for ornately filed beauty since 1950). The Super Legend was the perfect custom bike, being made to measure for the customer. These individual touches include the chrome-plated segment of the seat tube, which was treated first before being welded into place. The bike featured here is number 23843 – one of only 120 Super Legends ever made.

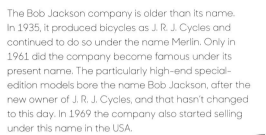

# BOB JACKSON
## Tricycle
### SUPPORTING WHEELS
### AS STANDARD FEATURE

**VARIETY**
RACING, CURIOSITY

**COUNTRY**
UNITED KINGDOM

**DATE**
1995

**WEIGHT**
13.3 KG (29.3 LB)

**FRAME**
VARNISHED STEEL, 55 CM (21.7 IN.)

**GEARS**
2 × 7, DERAILLEURSHIMANO DURA-ACE

**BRAKES**
RIM CENTRE PULL WEINMANN (FRONT I),
RIM CANTILEVER SHIMANO (FRONT II)

**TYRES**
27 IN. TUBULAR (FRONT),
2 × 27 IN. TUBULAR (REAR)

For anyone who thought the elaborate lugs of the Hetchins' top model, Magnum Opus, were not eye-catching enough, a third wheel could be added to make a tricycle that could be used for any situation, including competition riding.

Tricycles are not as stable as they might first appear; they are prone to veer off entirely without warning with inexperienced riders. They remain popular, however, and Bob Jackson tricycles are still available, as exclusive and high quality as ever. The tricycles are mostly based on the traditional bikes by Hetchins, the brand that merged with Bob Jackson in 1986. They have exquisite lugs, and parts remain handcrafted to customer requirements. Only one piece of this custom lugged model was ever produced (shown here). The tricycle featured is number 21999. (See Bob Jackson Super Legend on page 96.)

# ONE OFF
## Moulton Special
### A UNIQUE PIECE MADE OF TITANIUM

**VARIETY**
RACING, CURIOSITY

**COUNTRY**
USA / UNITED KINGDOM

**DATE**
1991

**WEIGHT**
9.6 KG (21.2 LB)

**FRAME**
TITANIUM, 56.8 CM (22.4 IN.) HIGH

**GEARS**
2 × 7, DERAILLEUR MAVIC 862

**BRAKES**
RIM SIDE PULL SCOTT
SUPER BRAKE

**TYRES**
17 IN. WIRED

Alex Moulton, who developed bicycles with small wheels and rubber suspensions, comes from the car business: he invented very similar suspensions for the classic Mini and many other British Leyland/Austin Rover cars. From the 1960s onwards he focused on the revolutionary Moulton bikes.

Mike Augspurger's company One Off in Florence, Massachusetts, specializes in producing unique, made-to-measure pieces. This includes not only bicycles, for example, but also wheelchairs. The common denominator in these products is the material; One Off favours titanium, thought to be the most promising for future high-end bicycles.

In 1991 Mike Augspurger made the acquaintance of Alex Moulton. Their friendship was deepened through cycling trips, and the next One Off idea developed. Augspurger wanted to produce a Moulton AM from titanium with a frame that could not be separated, and his friend supported the project and supplied special Moulton parts.

Only a couple of months later the new frame stood on the weighing scales. It proved to be 500 grams (1.1 lb) lighter than a Moulton AM Speed stainless-steel frame but likewise could not be separated.

Alex Moulton was rather cautious and agreed to no further experiments of this kind.

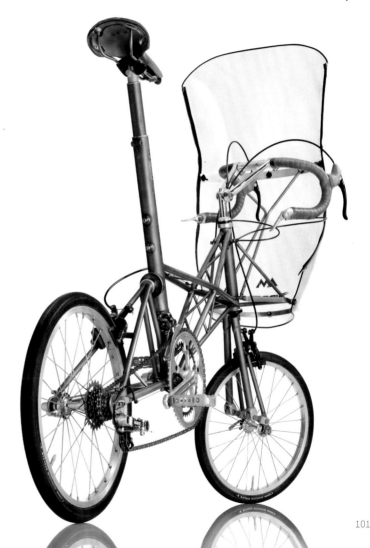

101

# ALEX MOULTON
## Speedsix
### WORLD RECORD
### FOR THE LITTLE MAN

**VARIETY**
RACING, TOURING

**COUNTRY**
UNITED KINGDOM

**DATE**
c. 1965

**WEIGHT**
13.3 KG (29.3 LB)

**FRAME**
VARNISHED STEEL, 50 CM (19.7 IN.) HIGH

**GEARS**
6, DERAILLEUR CAMPAGNOLO
GRAN SPORT (REAR)

**BRAKES**
RIM SIDE PULL WEINMANN TYPE 730

**TYRES**
17 IN. WIRED

Although the Moulton Speedsix was never publicly available in white, the colour has significance. In September 1967 the British cyclist Vic Nicholson broke the 1962 world record for cycling from Cardiff to London on a white Moulton 'S' Speed. However, since the route had been shortened by completion of the Severn Bridge in 1966, there now exist in fact two records from Cardiff to London: Woodburn's 1962 record can never be smashed because of the new route.

Record attempts were naturally set to influence the series models and might be the reason why the owner of this Speedsix changed the paint colour to white – as an homage to the 'S' speed.

At the end of the 1960s the 6-speed gear system was an unusual phenomenon, making the Moulton Speedsix twice as exotic. It was ahead of its time in its gear-shift technology, although in its design it was very contemporary.

The Moultons from the first years of production were rather unexciting mass-market goods, but with the leap to high-end, small series production in the 1980s their street credentials went up. The bicycle shown here is one of only 600 or so built, and is number K65310046.

# SØLLING Pedersen
## TIMELESS FOR MORE THAN A HUNDRED YEARS

**VARIETY**
URBAN

**COUNTRY**
DENMARK

**DATE**
1978

**WEIGHT**
11.9 KG (26.2 LB)

**FRAME**
VARNISHED STEEL, MEDIUM HEIGHT

**GEARS**
3, HUB GEAR TORPEDO (REAR)

**BRAKES**
RIM SIDE PULL ALTENBURGER SYNCHRON (FRONT),
COASTER BRAKE (REAR)

**TYRES**
28 IN. WIRED

Mikael Pedersen (1855–1929) was a Danish blacksmith and musician with a talent for innovation. He invented an eclectic mix of mechanisms, including a threshing machine to separate the wheat from the chaff, a gearing system for horse-driven mills and a braking system for carriages. Most interestingly he rethought the bicycle, focusing on creating a frame that could fit any height of rider. His design was primarily concerned with a flexible saddle, which he suspended using a plastic-coated steel cord. When the rider sat down, the bike gained stability as a result of tensile loading on its thin, light tubes.

Pedersen's original design dates from the 1890s, and in its first life (before World War I) the Pedersen was built in Dursley in the UK. Its second life began in Denmark around 1978, with prototypes such as the Sølling Pedersen that remain in series production today.

# WILHELMINA PLAST Itera
## ART AND PLASTIC

**VARIETY**
RACING, CURIOSITY

**COUNTRY**
SWEDEN

**DATE**
1984

**WEIGHT**
18.3 KG (40.3 LB)

**FRAME**
PLASTIC,
56.6 CM (22.3 IN.) HIGH

**GEARS**
2 × 5, DERAILLEUR
CAMPAGNOLO 980

**BRAKES**
RIM SIDE PULL CLB

**TYRES**
27 IN. WIRED

If there were a prize for the most bizarre bicycle ever constructed, then the Wilhelmina Plast Itera would win gold.

Manufactured in Sweden, almost all of the components were made from plastic – resulting in a bicycle that warped in hot summer weather and compromised braking. There was no apparent weight advantage with the plastic, and the tyres also proved an anomaly, being one millimetre larger than standard size.

The money to develop this bicycle originally came from the Swedish National Bank, and in 1980 the first model came out on the market. The bicycle was delivered to the customer in pieces in a box, with special tools supplied to construct it. But before the Itera even hit the road the manufacturer received complaints, as many of the boxes arrived incomplete, the kits missing vital parts.

Racing models of the Wilhemina Plast Itera were very rare, but the antique pink colour was perfect for a bicycle which seemed conspicuously lacking in seriousness.

# CAPO Elite 'Eis'
## A STRANGE HYBRID

**VARIETY**
SINGLESPEED, CURIOSITY

**COUNTRY**
AUSTRIA

**DATE**
c. 1966

**WEIGHT**
11 KG (24.3 LB)

**FRAME**
VARNISHED STEEL,
56.5 CM (22.2 IN.) HIGH

**GEAR**
1, FIXED

**TYRES**
26 IN. WIRED

The successful cross between an ice skate and a bicycle, the Capo Elite 'Eis' is an extraordinary creation. It has a rear tyre accessorized with metal spikes to provide propulsion and a skid at the front to provide better steering. These are designed to ensure absolute directional stability and reduce the chance of slippage. The only danger was that in an accident a rider had to hope he or she would avoid the spiked rear wheel.

Even in Austria, where the 'Eis' was manufactured, the ice bike had only a modest distribution. The bicycle featured here is in fact unique, having been customized further by its previous owner. The manufacturer Capo was renowned for another of its bicycles, the 'Computer Bike', where the computer was able to calculate the optimum frame geometry. Capo was founded by two professional cyclists, Otto and Walter Cap in 1930 – the former had been Austrian national champion in the 1920s.

# RABENEICK
## CYCLING AS AN
## ART FORM

**VARIETY**
SINGLESPEED, CURIOSITY

**COUNTRY**
AUSTRIA

**DATE**
c. 1955

**WEIGHT**
12.3 KG (27.1 LB)

**FRAME**
VARNISHED STEEL,
53 CM (20.9 IN.) HIGH

**GEAR**
1, FIXED

**TYRES**
26 IN. WIRED

By the mid-1950s, 41 German national championship titles had already been won on Rabeneick bikes. This was not surprising given that Rabeneick also kept a professional racing team and the indoor cycling sports – named Saalsport in German – were a side project, albeit a primarily aesthetic one. Manoeuvrability counted in Saalsport and the gear ratio of these bikes is 1:1 (which meant riding quickly on them was impossible). Because of the fixed wheel, however, it was possible to ride backwards, and the position of the handlebars and seat really helped when doing 'wheelies'.

Rabeneick was founded by August Rabeneick in 1930 in Brackwede near Bielefeld, Germany. The company was responsible for producing the most popular bicycles for indoor cycling sports, particularly in the immediate period post-World War II.

Saalsport had become established in the late 19th century, at a time when cycling clubs were still incredibly elitist. The pursuit was aimed less at sporting success and more at enjoying spending time with peers in a club atmosphere. As bicycles became cheaper at the beginning of the 20th century, the general public could afford to buy one. Sporting competitions thus opened up, becoming entertainment for the masses.

Cycling competitions were held in the halls of guest houses and inns, particularly in winter. They included races with bicycles on rollers (using a contraption with three rollers to cycle on the spot), circus-like performances, creative cycling and round-dance cycling. It was even possible to play at pivoting on the extensions of the hub axle nuts while the bike rode on. This playful use of the bicycle was reflected in the design, with tyres made a light brown so that no skid marks could be left on the hall floor.

The bicycle featured here is number 171680.

# WORLDSCAPE CO. LTD
## Aitelen Chainless
### THREE TIMES LUCKY

**VARIETY**
URBAN, CURIOSITY

**COUNTRY**
TAIWAN

**DATE**
c. 1992

**WEIGHT**
15.8 KG (34.8 LB)

**FRAME**
VARNISHED STEEL,
50.6 CM (19.9 IN.) HIGH

**GEARS**
5, HUB GEAR SACHS
PENTASPORT (REAR)

**BRAKES**
RIM V-BRAKE
SHIMANO DEORE LX

**TYRES**
28 IN. WIRED

Over one hundred years ago, the Frenchman Gaston Rivière won the Bordeaux-Paris race three consecutive times (1896, 1897 and 1898) on a chainless shaft-driven bike. Shortly after 1900 France saw the first multi-speed shaft drive, and around the same time shaft-driven bicycles were combined with 2- or 3-speed hub gears in the USA.

The concept then was left dormant for many decades to be revitalized with the creation of the Aitelen Chainless bicycle. It came with technical refinements so the straight toothing became helical, and then hypoid.

With efficiency still an issue, however, the traditional chain-drive bicycle need not fear for its future. The shaft drive of this Aitelen Chainless is one of its exemplary parts; made with the utmost precision, it is a joy to use - along with the famous Torpedo 5-speed gears. Unfortunately, the frame does not deliver the same high specification, having been welded without lugs in an average fashion. The bicycle shown is number TC97A00047.

# ALENAX TRB 250
# SQUARING
# THE CIRCLE

VARIETY
URBAN, CURIOSITY

COUNTRY
TAIWAN

DATE
c. 1988

WEIGHT
18 KG (39.9 LB)

FRAME
VARNISHED STEEL,
49 CM (19.3 IN.) HIGH

GEARS
ADJUSTABLE

BRAKES
RIM SIDE PULL DIA COMPE

TYRES
27 IN. WIRED

Ideas on ways to substitute a circular pedalling motion with an alternative movement or mechanism are numerous in the history of bicycling. As early as 1880 the Star penny farthing worked to the same principle (having a small wheel at the front, reducing the risk of falling off over the handlebars). In 1893 the Swedish firm Svea unveiled a similar concept, as did Terrot in France with his Levocyclette in 1900. The Jaray recumbent bicycle of the 1920s was moved by a lever drive, so no pedalling was involved.

The Alenax TRB 250 continues this tradition of alternative motion with its transbars driving a chain; this in turn engages in sprockets, so the rider can freewheel if they choose. These sprockets are mounted to the left and right of the rear wheel hub. Even though the system offers various gears, it is not really usable due to the clearly noticeable dead centres during the crank rotation while pedalling. Even with a conventional drive they are unpleasant, and could not be mitigated by PMP cranks (see the C.B.T. Italia Champions on page 184) and the Colrout (see Gazelle Champion Mondial, page 180).

# GEBRÜDER HEIDEMANN
## High Touring
## Super 30 Inch
BIG IS BEAUTIFUL

**VARIETY**
TOURING, CURIOSITY

**COUNTRY**
WEST GERMANY

**DATE**
c. 1983

**WEIGHT**
18.1 KG (39.9 LB)

**FRAME**
STEEL VARNISHED, 63.5 CM (25 IN.) HIGH

**GEARS**
5, HUB GEAR TORPEDO (REAR)

**BRAKES**
DRUM BRAKE (FRONT),
COASTER BRAKE (REAR)

**TYRES**
30 IN. WIRED

116

From a distance the Gebrüder Heidemann High Touring Super 30 inch appeared to be a robust touring bike. Its substantial size was even more impressive close up.

The frame of the Super 30 inch was 63.5 centimetres in height, and was reinforced with a second top tube, making it a good match for tall cyclists.

What merits attention and earned this bicycle its name were its 30-inch wheels. These not only maintained the well-loved proportions of a touring bike, but also convinced a rider of its real advantages. The larger a wheel, the less it fell into potholes, while an increase in wheelbase meant improvement in directional stability and a steady rotation. Inevitable disadvantages to larger wheels were the increase in weight and the greater force needed to set the wheels in rotation – these bikes were a real workout to start! And as the years passed and the unusual tyres needed to be replaced, new ones (produced especially for this bicycle) became harder to find.

The number of the Super 30 inch featured is 306/867099.

# RALEIGH
## Tourist
SHINY HAPPY
CYCLE

RALEIGH TOURIST (GENTLEMEN)

**VARIETY**
URBAN

**COUNTRY**
UNITED KINGDOM

**DATE**
c. 1970

**WEIGHT**
20.9 KG (46.1 LB)

**FRAME**
CHROMED STEEL,
57.3 CM (22.6 IN.) HIGH

**GEARS**
3, HUB GEAR TORPEDO
(REAR)

**BRAKES**
RIM ROD BRAKE

**TYRES**
28 IN. WIRED (635)

RALEIGH TOURIST (LADIES)

**VARIETY**
URBAN

**COUNTRY**
UNITED KINGDOM

**DATE**
c. 1970

**WEIGHT**
19.8 KG (43.7 LB)

**FRAME**
CHROMED STEEL,
56.2 CM (22.1 IN.) HIGH

**GEARS**
3, HUB GEAR STURMEY
ARCHER (REAR)

**BRAKES**
RIM ROD BRAKE

**TYRES**
28 IN. WIRED (635)

The appearance of the chrome-plated frame of the Raleigh Tourist bicycle lends it a promising air of lightness, but appearances can be deceptive and it is heavier on the road. On the other hand, the robust, beautiful Tourist is perfect for family outings, with the gentlemen's version boasting an integrated child seat.

The batteries for the stationary lights are accommodated inside the channel of the seat tube, and the fully enclosed chain means that the bicycle can handle rough weather – highly appropriate as the Tourist originated in the United Kingdom.

Shortly after 1900 rod brakes, such as the ones on the Raleigh Tourist, became a national treasure, and the vast majority of bicycles in India still have them today.

The Raleigh Tourist is also remarkable for the complete absence of aluminium. The slogan on the chain case, dating from before 1900, read 'The All-Steel Bicycle' – with steel an important product of the Industrial Revolution, this was something to be proud of. Today, though, the slogan is no longer used.

# TRUSSARDI
## WAR AND PEACE

**VARIETY**
URBAN, FOLDING

**COUNTRY**
ITALY

**DATE**
1983

**WEIGHT**
19.1 KG (42.1 LB)

**FRAME**
VARNISHED STEEL, 54 CM (21.3 IN.) HIGH

**GEARS**
3, HUB GEAR TORPEDO (REAR)

**BRAKES**
RIM SIDE PULL UNIVERSAL

**TYRES**
28 IN. WIRED

One of the few folding bicycles with 28-inch wheels, this model significantly improved its suitability for long distance and bad roads. The design was similar to the BSA Paratrooper, a bicycle specifically designed for paratroopers in World War II (see page 218).

The bicycle was also used in peacetime. In 1983 the fashion company Trussardi took it on to dress it up in civilian colours. The new-look Trussardi was decorated with plenty of leather and came with smart saddlebags, which could also be carried as shoulder bags by the owner. Trussardi produced around 3,000 of these fashionable bicycles.

Around the same time Trussardi began refining other items, from refitting car interiors to internal aircraft fittings, which reflected well on their luxury brand image.

# UMBERTO DEI
## Giubileo
THE WAY WE
USED TO RIDE

**VARIETY**
URBAN

**COUNTRY**
ITALY

**DATE**
1996

**WEIGHT**
18.2 KG (40.1 LB)

**FRAME**
STEEL VARNISHED,
57 CM (22.4 IN.) HIGH

**GEARS**
3, HUB GEAR TORPEDO (REAR)

**BRAKES**
RIM SIDE PULL
URSUSS SUPER LUXE

**TYRES**
28 IN. WIRED

Umberto Dei has been involved in the bicycle market since 1896, so it has a wealth of experience. The company celebrated its centenary by launching a high-end city bicycle, the Giubileo. Made by hand, it had exquisite leather handles, a sprung leather seat, leather rear wheel cover and even little saddlebags. The women's bike also came with a large shopping basket at the front. The bike shown here is number 16275C.

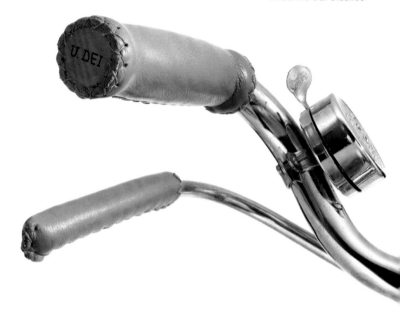

The brand had its beginnings in racing bicycles and – despite the limited financial means of its founder – Dei managed quickly to establish a reputation as an innovative, modern constructor of light racing bikes early in the 20th century. Dei refined components to preserve the quality but decrease the weight, recognizing that light wheels were both more manoeuvrable and required less force to rotate. Umberto Dei's wheels measured just 68 centimetres (26.8 inches) in diameter and they were slimmer too, which makes them forerunners of the contemporary tubular tyres that are standard today.

# HERSKIND + HERSKIND
## Copenhagen
POETRY IN MOTION

**VARIETY**
URBAN

**COUNTRY**
DENMARK

**DATE**
c. 1995

**WEIGHT**
12 KG (26.5 LB)

**FRAME**
VARNISHED STEEL,
54.5 CM (21.4 IN.) HIGH

**GEARS**
3, HUB GEAR TORPEDO (REAR)

**BRAKES**
COASTER BRAKE (REAR)

**TYRES**
28 IN. WIRED

The Copenhagen originated in Denmark, a country that is not traditionally associated with racing cyclists. Perhaps as a result this bicycle did not appear until one of its designers, Jan Herskind, relocated to Germany.

Herskind was born in 1955 in Roskilde, Denmark, and studied theatre before turning to the design world in the mid-1970s. He designed products such as the world clock (which for a period kept time in the lobby of the Museum of Modern Art in New York) and, together with his brother, Jakob Herskind, he also designed clothes and the Copenhagen bicycle. They produced different models, including a women's bike and a cargo bike, and they were all limited editions, produced strictly by hand with no assembly lines. The bicycle featured is number 1663, and is a limited designer edition of which only 500 pieces were produced.

The Copenhagen is a captivating visual mix. Dark paintwork contrasts with light natural materials of leather (such as the seat with artistically sewn handles) and wood (the mudguards, pedals and even the narrow chain guard).

# TUR MECCANICA
## Bi Bici
## A SHORT BICYCLE MADE FOR TWO

**VARIETY**
TANDEM, CURIOSITY

**COUNTRY**
ITALY

**DATE**
c. 1980

**WEIGHT**
22.5 KG (49.6 LB)

**FRAME**
VARNISHED STEEL,
43.2 CM (17 IN.) HIGH

**GEARS**
4, DERAILLEUR HURET (REAR)

**BRAKES**
RIM SIDE PULL
UNIVERSAL DRUM BRAKE

**TYRES**
26 IN. WIRED

A major disadvantage of most tandem bicycles is that their manoeuvrability is severely compromised. The long wheelbase suits distance cycling on straight roads, but narrow, winding lanes are out of the question.

Anyone wishing to find a less traditional tandem design in 1980 needed to look no further than Tur Meccanica's Bi Bici. Measuring only marginally longer than a single bike, it did not require the rider to change either their route or cycling style – with the exception of the cardinal tandem rule that the stoker mounts last. The presence of the captain on the front prevented the bike suddenly tipping back, which might occur if the stoker mounted first.

The risk of a sudden 'wheelie' was only present when riding this shorter tandem if the stoker was much heavier in weight than the captain. The Bi Bici, for this reason, was rather more suitable for riding with children, or for two slim, equal-weighted adults.

It was also a worthy model to study for its engineering skill; the rear bottom bracket spindle passed through the rear wheel hub but did not drive it. The force instead was diverted via a chain to the captain's transmission, and from there diverted again down the right-hand side to the rear wheel hub. A derailleur allowed drivers to choose from four gears.

The short tandem design dates back as far as the 1880s, when they were produced with a similar frame geometry and traditional solo bicycle wheelbase.

# BUDDY BIKE
## Buddy Bike
EQUALITY ON
ONE BIKE

**VARIETY**
TANDEM, CURIOSITY

**COUNTRY**
TAIWAN

**DATE**
c. 1988

**WEIGHT**
27.5 KG (60.6 LB)

**FRAME**
VARNISHED STEEL, 46 CM (18.1 IN.) HIGH

**GEARS**
6, DERAILLEUR SHIMANO ALTUS (REAR)

**BRAKES**
RIM SIDE PULL ODYSSEY (FRONT),
RIM CENTRE PULL ODYSSEY PITBULL (REAR)

**TYRES**
26 IN. WIRED

The friendly concept of the Buddy Bike was first thought of before 1900, and there have been several versions since. The number of the bicycle shown here is B003557. It was the tandem for riders who prioritized socializing over performance, with the arrangement of the seats making communication easy, and prompting a nickname – 'the sociable'.

The Buddy Bike gave the left-hand passenger only the power of steering, although its format allowed riders to debate and agree on the direction of travel. The handlebars on the right were just for balance.

Most importantly, the Buddy Bike required a balanced load to avoid the bike tilting or falling sideways. This meant both passengers needed to have equal weights and should, if possible, refrain from quarrelling during travel. Using the Buddy Bike solo was not an option as the offset seats made balance impossible – unless you only cycled around left-hand bends!

# HASE SPEZIALRÄDER
## Pino Tour
## FOR A LAID-BACK RIDE

**VARIETY**
TANDEM, TOURING

**COUNTRY**
GERMANY

**DATE**
2010

**WEIGHT**
23.8 KG (52.5 LB)

**FRAME**
VARNISHED ALUMINIUM, 47.5 CM (18.7 IN.) HIGH

**GEARS**
3 × 9, DERAILLEUR SHIMANO DURA-ACE TRIPLE (FRONT),
DERAILLEUR SHIMANO DEORE XT (REAR)

**BRAKES**
DISC BRAKE MAGURA LOUISE

**TYRES**
20 IN. WIRED (FRONT),
26 IN. WIRED TYRE (BACK)

The position of the stoker on the back is arguably more boring than the captain's, who can enjoy the unobscured vista in front. Another disadvantage of being the stoker is that you have no braking or steering power – nor are any wishes communicated to the captain in front likely to be heard in the wind.

Traditional tandems don't exactly make communication easy, and this is an aspect that the Hase company tried to improve with their Pino Tour bicycle. The two tandem seats are here set much closer to one another, putting the front rider in a recumbent position and allowing the upright stoker to enjoy an unrestricted view behind. Communication is easy, and the tandem can be finely adjusted to the length of the captain's legs.

The short 140-centimetre (55-inch) wheelbase ensures manoeuvrability, and the captain can take a breather from pedalling and rest his or her feet on a free wheel.

The aluminium frame can be taken apart, and when disassembled the Pino Tour measures 110 × 30 × 80 centimetres (43.3 × 11.8 × 31.5 inches). Hase produced around 2,300 pieces of this design.

The company has built specialist bicycles since 1994. All of the firm's employees are avid cyclists, including director Marec Hase. He began producing bicycle prototypes as early as 13 years old, and by the time he won the 'Jugend forscht' (Germany's competition for aspiring young scientists) Hase had already built 30 bicycles. He established his company at the age of 23.

# SHORT–BIKE 3R
## PULLING POWER

**VARIETY**
CARGO, CURIOSITY

**COUNTRY**
GERMANY

**DATE**
1996

**WEIGHT**
30.1 KG (66.4 LB)

**FRAME**
STAINLESS STEEL + PLASTIC,
54 CM (21.3 IN.) HIGH

**GEARS**
3, HUB GEAR TORPEDO (FRONT)

**BRAKES**
DRUM BRAKE SACHS (FRONT I),
RIM SIDE PULL (FRONT II)

**TYRES**
20 IN. WIRED (FRONT),
2 × 16 IN. WIRED (REAR)

To take the Short-Bike 3R out into heavy traffic would take a good deal of confidence, and there is ample room for that in this bold design.

The payload on the surface between the rear wheels is up to 60 kilograms (132.2 lb). It has a stable construction, and its significant weight gives the rider an enormously effective workout.

On the other hand, the Short-Bike offers a great many real advantages. They include an extremely comfortable broad seat, with backrest set in an ergonomic position, manoeuvrability and an enviably neat turning circle. These allow the rider to speed away, even when there are only three gears. Anyone living in a windy or hilly area could opt for the 7-gear version with roller brakes, while for the rider who wants the bicycle to do all the work, there is the 7-gear model with electric drive.

Incidentally the Short-Bike can be split by lifting a bolt and separating the back part with the wheels from the front part. This makes the bike even more compact for transport.

# SMITH & CO.
# Long John
## A WORKING
## DAY ON WHEELS

**VARIETY**
CARGO, CURIOSITY

**COUNTRY**
DENMARK

**DATE**
c. 1983

**WEIGHT**
32 KG (70.5 LB)

**FRAME**
VARNISHED STEEL, 50 CM (19.9 IN.) HIGH

**GEARS**
3, HUB GEAR TORPEDO (REAR)

**BRAKES**
DRUM BRAKE WEINMANN (FRONT),
COASTER BRAKE TORPEDO (REAR)

**TYRES**
20 IN. WIRED (FRONT), 23 IN. WIRED (REAR)

Bicycles designed for transporting loads have seldom been objects of beauty. Packages were traditionally placed into luggage racks at the front and rear, and specific cargo baskets were used when heavy cargo needed to be transported – usually requiring the addition of a third wheel.

The Long John by Smith & Co. was the only two-wheeled cargo bike. It was also the longest, with a load capacity of around 140 kilograms (308.6 lb) including the rider. Even when fully laden it was easy to balance, leaving passers-by in disbelief. When fully loaded, the Long John tended to draw spectators particularly on embarkation and launch and produced awe from other cyclists when it proceeded to overtake at speed.

Particularly noteworthy is the well-conceived steering design, which passes underneath the cargo area, elegantly bypassing the front wheel when it pivots.

The Long John design has historically been produced by various makers in a range of countries. This Danish model is by Smith & Co. and is number S119199V.

# SIRONVAL
# Sportplex
## A RECLINING
## BIKE FOR ONE

**VARIETY**
TOURING, CURIOSITY

**COUNTRY**
FRANCE

**DATE**
1939

**WEIGHT**
20 KG (44.1 LB)

**FRAME**
VARNISHED STEEL, ADJUSTABLE HEIGHT

**GEARS**
3, DERAILLEUR SIMPLEX TOURISTE (REAR)

**BRAKES**
RIM SIDE PULL

**TYRES**
22 IN. WIRED TYRE (FRONT),
24 IN. WIRED (REAR)

144

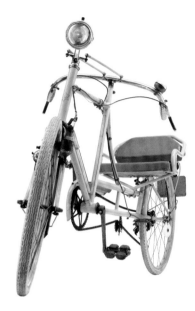

and the excellent support given to the rider by the backrest. Recumbent bikes nevertheless continued to be popular among those who cycled as a hobby, although the number of Sironval Sportplex bikes sold remained low, at around 200.

The sensational thing about the Sportplex model featured is that it is in mint condition with only slight patination. The number plate, required during the German occupation of France in World War II, suggests that the Sironval Sportplex has spent post-war decades safely protected from weather and traffic.

At first glance the Sironval Sportplex looks like a tandem. On closer inspection, however, it is a recumbent bike for one cyclist.

In France, recumbent bicycles were in vogue in the 1930s. Attention was fixed on designers Charles and Georges Mochet, who in 1933 attempted to break the world hour record (set earlier by Oscar Egg) with their recumbent design. They were successful, and although the rider, Francis Faure, was something of an unknown before the record (45.056 km/h), he certainly wasn't afterwards.

At the following UCI conference, the governing body reacted by banning recumbent bicycles from taking part in races. The designs were, after all, superior to the traditional diamond frames – the result of improved aerodynamics

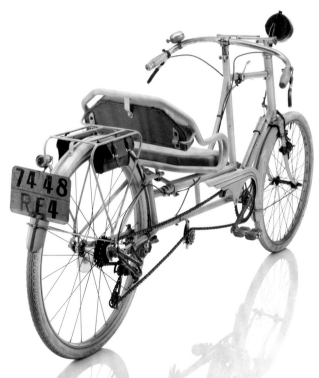

# KÖTHKE
## BY SPECIALISTS
## FOR SPECIALISTS

**VARIETY**
RACING, SINGLESPEED, TANDEM

**COUNTRY**
GERMANY

**DATE**
c. 1948

**WEIGHT**
19.5 KG (43 LB)

**FRAME**
VARNISHED STEEL,
54.8 CM (21.6 IN.) HIGH

**GEAR**
1, FIXED

**TYRES**
27 IN. TUBULAR

146

What the frame builder Faliero Masi achieved in Italy was managed years before by Fritz Köthke near Cologne in Germany. Köthke's frames were ordered by the best professionals and amateurs around the world, to be painted in their racing colours. The Italian cyclist Alfredo Binda won the 1928 world road championships on a Köthke frame painted with a Mifa (Middle German Bicycle Factory public company) design. Fritz's brother, Heinrich Köthke, was responsible for the sales; he was also the leaseholder of the nearby racing track for many years. This exposed a steady stream of people to Köthke's bikes, resulting in his shop becoming the meeting place for active racing cyclists and sportsmen.

The Köthke model featured here has a track tandem frame and was built for one Eduard Lachnit, a bicycle dealer (and himself a frame builder) in Vienna. Lachnit painted the frame in the colours of his own Elan brand, and made it available to the racing cyclists at the Vienna Velodrome. Its wins are unrecorded.

# LABOR
## Spéciale Course
### A BICYCLE BRIDGE

**VARIETY**
RACING

**COUNTRY**
FRANCE

**DATE**
1922

**WEIGHT**
12.3 KG (27.1 LB)

**FRAME**
VARNISHED STEEL,
57.5 CM (22.6 IN.) HIGH

**GEARS**
1 + 1, FIXED

**BRAKES**
RIM SIDE PULL (REAR)

**TYRES**
27 IN. TUBULAR

The history of Labor bicycles is somewhat unclear, although it is known that in 1906 and 1907 Louis Darragon became both the world stayer racing champion and French national stayer champion on a Labor. The company was bought by Alcyon, the classic motorbike manufacturer, in the 1920s.

In the 1920s Labor bicycles were renowned for being particularly torsion-resistant and advertisements from the time (showing a classroom of monkeys drawing Labor bicycles) acquired cult status.

A familiar characteristic of a Labor bicycle was the truss bridge design on the frame, inspired by bridge engineering, to which they ascribed its rigidity. Popular in the USA on Iver Johnson bicycles, which perhaps inspired the French models, it had been around since 1902. Labor racing bikes were, therefore, destined to thrive in the cobbled classic Paris–Roubaix race, with Paul Deman winning in 1920 and Albert Dejonghe in 1922. Further victories followed in the Bordeaux–Paris race and the Tour of Morocco, while Labor also launched the professional career of François Faber, one of the most successful racing cyclists before World War I.

The Labor model featured below (number 104040) is in mint condition, and impresses by hardly twisting when ridden.

# CAMINADE CAMINARGENT
## Bordeaux–Paris
TOO DELICATE
FOR THIS WORLD

**VARIETY**
RACING

**COUNTRY**
FRANCE

**DATE**
1937

**WEIGHT**
8.3 KG (18.3 LB)

**FRAME**
ALUMINIUM, 57.3 CM (22.6 IN.) HIGH

**GEAR**
1

**BRAKES**
RIM SIDE PULL SPORT BOWDEN TOURISTE

**TYRES**
27 IN. TUBULAR

In the 19th century there were many attempts to reduce the weight of a bicycle through the use of aluminium parts. In London and Paris, frames were cast in aluminium, and drilled to make them hollow, but these experiments on the whole failed, and few examples have survived.

The Caminargent bicycle, created in the 1930s, was more successful. Its octagonal aluminium tubes were housed in finely detailed lugs of a baroque design. However, the bicycle still liked to twist despite the screws employed to strengthen the frame, and with compromised integrity fine tears could appear.

The few surviving Carminargent bikes should therefore be ridden gently, and only on special occasions.

153

# W. & R. BAINES V.S. 37
## RIDING THE GARDEN GATE!

**VARIETY**
RACING, CURIOSITY

**COUNTRY**
UNITED KINGDOM

**DATE**
c. 1947

**WEIGHT**
9.8 KG (21.6 LB)

**FRAME**
VARNISHED STEEL,
56 CM (22 IN.) HIGH

**GEAR**
1 + 1, FIXED

**BRAKES**
RIM SIDE PULL GB HIDUMINIUM

**TYRES**
27 IN. TUBULAR

This British classic was designed in the 1930s by Reg Baines who, together with his brother Willie, had worked in their factory since 1919. The V.S. 37 entered series production by 1934.

With the number '37' referring to the size of the wheelbase in inches, it gave an idea of this short bike's manoeuvrability. Aside from its uninspired name, the V.S. 37 was also nicknamed the Whirlwind and then the Flying Gate, which subsequently stuck.

Its numerous frame tubes might have looked random, but they made for good manoeuvrability and a superbly rigid frame.

The Flying Gate is far better to ride than to look at, and replicas are still being built to this day by T. J. Cycles.

# AUSTRO-DAIMLER Vent Noir & STEYR-DAIMLER-PUCH Vent Noir
## EQUALITY ON THE ROAD

**AUSTRO-DAIMLER VENT NOIR**
**(GENTLEMEN; ABOVE)**

**VARIETY** TOURING

**COUNTRY** AUSTRIA

**DATE** 1978

**WEIGHT** 10.4 KG (22.9 LB)

**FRAME** VARNISHED STEEL,
55.8 CM (22 IN.) HIGH

**GEARS** 2 × 5, DERAILLEUR
SHIMANO DURA-ACE

**BRAKES** RIM SIDE PULL
SHIMANO DURA-ACE

**TYRES** 27 IN. TUBULAR

**STEYR-DAIMLER-PUCH VENT NOIR**
**(LADIES; PAGE 161)**

**VARIETY** TOURING

**COUNTRY** AUSTRIA

**DATE** 1978

**WEIGHT** 10.4 KG (22.9 LB)

**FRAME** VARNISHED STEEL,
57.5 CM (22.6 IN.) HIGH

**GEARS** 2 × 5, DERAILLEUR
SHIMANO CRANE

**BRAKES** RIM SIDE PULL
SHIMANO DURA-ACE

**TYRES** 27 IN. TUBULAR

In 1978 the matt black Steyr-Daimler-Puch Vent Noir models barely attracted attention in top circles of cycle racing. The professional Puch cycling team was only launched in 1980, and back then the riders (including Joaquim Agostinho, Didi Thurau and Klaus-Peter Thaler) rolled on striking green Puch Mistral Ultimas.

Founded in 1889, Puch was one of the oldest manufacturers in Austria. Its aim around a century later was to gain a reputation for high-end bikes, using its Mistral series to lead the way. A dedicated design department was set up to this end in 1976. It reached top form with the prototype of a monocoque frame, similar to the Lotus Sport 110 (see page 72) and the Biomega MN01 (see page 66), designed by Ferdinand Alexander Porsche.

Although sold in Austria under the name Puch, the bicycles were renamed for export markets as Steyr-Daimler-Puch or Austro-Daimler, and they remain distinguished names today.

With the colour of its frame, the Vent Noir series invoked the ideal of contemporary sporty shades with anodized gold rims, and the most expensive black Dura-Ace components in the Shimano programme. (Lotus John Player Special Formula 1 team of the time also used a combination of black and gold.)

In 1980 the matt black paintwork of the Vent Noir models turned into a smoked-chrome finish, which was later adopted by the C.B.T. Italia Champions bicycle (see page 184).

# SELECT
# Campionissimo
## A RARE BREED

**VARIETY**
TOURING

**COUNTRY**
AUSTRIA

**DATE**
c. 1978

**WEIGHT**
8.2 KG (18.1 LB)

**FRAME**
VARNISHED STEEL,
53.7 CM (21.1 IN.) HIGH

**GEARS**
2 × 5, DERAILLEUR
CAMPAGNOLO RALLY

**BRAKES**
RIM SIDE PULL CLB

**TYRES**
27 IN. TUBULAR

The letter 'S' delicately soldered into the frame could be mistaken for the brand, Select, but in fact identified the frame builder. In the 1970s Michael 'Mischa' Steinkellner worked as a taxi-driver, but on occasion, if a customer requested, he would weld a particularly exquisite bicycle frame with light, refined lugs.

His men's racing bike frames were rare and a women's frame rarer still. This bicycle, with the Columbus SL tubes (Super Leggera meaning 'super light') and CLB brakes that at the time were second to none, may even be a unique piece. It has number 7838 on the frame. Other bicycles in the Select range were considerably more common.

The company, whose premises were located on Lerchenfelder Gürtel in Vienna, was one of Austria's oldest. The bicycles became famous in the 1930s through to the 1950s. Numerous races were won on the mainly yellow racing bikes. In the 1960s success continued for Select bicycles with only the paint colour changing. After the 1960s more and more frames were made in Italy and labelled Select, rather than being manufactured in Vienna. From the 1980s onwards Select, like many other companies, was a bicycle dealer. In 2004 the shop and company closed for good.

# ZEUS Zeus
## A GREEK GOD FROM SPAIN

**VARIETY**
RACING

**COUNTRY**
SPAIN

**DATE** 1979

**WEIGHT**
9.9 KG (21.8 LB)

**FRAME**
VARNISHED STEEL,
55.7 CM (21.9 IN.) HIGH

**GEARS**
2 × 6, DERAILLEUR ZEUS 2000

**BRAKES**
RIM CENTRE PULL ZEUS 2000

**TYRES**
27 IN. TUBULAR

The Spanish company Zeus was always believed
to have taken inspiration from its Italian rival,
Campagnolo. Zeus was founded in 1926 by Don
Nicolás Arregui in Eibar in the Basque country, and
produced both components and frames. It was
not uncommon for a Zeus to emerge from the
Spanish factory complete, with hardly any additional
components having to be brought in.

Outside Spain, Zeus bicycles were often rumoured
to be poor quality, but in fact low labour costs meant
reasonably priced components, and sometimes even
more advanced technology. The aluminium sprockets
at the rear were incredibly light (though they did
wear out quickly), while the tubes for the top models
were from Reynolds. A Reynolds 531, the model that
became a benchmark for many decades, is featured
here. Its number is 174 CR. The design of the Zeus
2000 group and the company's use of titanium were
also years ahead of their time.

The low price was the only handicap. The mail
order dealer Brügelmann had to underscore the high
quality of Zeus in the late 1970s, when the top Zeus
model with lots of titanium parts cost approximately
half that of a Gianni Motta with Campagnolo Super
Record components.

# MASI
# Gran Criterium
## FRAME OF HEARTS

**VARIETY**
RACING

**COUNTRY**
ITALY

**DATE**
1978

**WEIGHT**
9.7 KG (21.4 LB)

**FRAME**
VARNISHED STEEL, 59.3 CM (23.3 IN.) HIGH

**GEARS**
2 × 6, DERAILLEUR CAMPAGNOLO SUPER RECORD

**BRAKES**
RIM SIDE PULL CAMPAGNOLO SUPER RECORD

**TYRES**
27 IN. TUBULAR

Many Masi frames carried a different name, with the designer Faliero Masi (a racing cyclist in younger years) producing frames for other professionals to be painted in the colours of their team's sponsor. This unwavering allegiance among riders was a credit to Masi's frames, which were excellent to ride and particularly light. Eddy Merckx began his career riding a Masi whose paintwork disguised it as a Peugeot, and his teammate Tom Simpson made the same choice. Rik van Looy's Masi was painted as a Superia, and Fausto Coppi, Jacques Anquetil and Vittorio Adorni also rode Masi frames in their time.

Faliero Masi was known as 'The Tailor', and in 1984 an American cycling magazine labelled him 'the Enzo Ferrari of frame building'.

The workshop where Masi produced the frames was small, and he used to close the shutters for some privacy. The one person always granted access was his son Alberto, the brains behind the many little refinements that even today make a Masi great.

Alberto Masi has seen the business through to its successful present. Today the Masi Gran Criterium bicycle is one of the most sought-after collectors' items. The 1978 model featured here was one of the last ever produced and is numbered HAT58486M.

# COLNAGO
## Brügelmann
A DESIGNER
MODEL

**VARIETY**
TOURING

**COUNTRY**
ITALY

**DATE**
c. 1979

**WEIGHT**
9.4 KG (20.7 LB)

**FRAME**
VARNISHED STEEL, 57 CM (22.4 LB)

**GEARS**
2 × 6, DERAILLEUR
CAMPAGNOLO NUOVO RECORD

**BRAKES**
RIM SIDE PULL CAMPAGNOLO

**TYRES**
27 IN. TUBULAR

The matt black engine bonnet of the Opel Manta made this shade and finish synonymous with all things sporty, and gold has always been considered a symbol of luxury. So it is natural that a deluxe Colnago bicycle would be painted in this prestigious livery.

The model featured was sold by bicycle dealers from Frankfurt am Main called Manfred and Rolf Brügelmann, who distributed the bicycles under their own name.

They opened a shop in 1932 and published an annual mail order catalogue – surpassed in size only by city phone directories. Their biggest successes came in the 1970s, lasting into the 1990s, and the company forged many strong relationships with well-known bicycle manufacturers. Ernesto Colnago liked to supply Brügelmann, as did Cino Cinelli, and customers could even fit their own bicycles at Brügelmann with particularly high-end parts.

Around 1980 'Brügelmann specialities' were presented in the catalogue – highly refined punched, pantographed, anodized and even gold-plated parts. Psychological tuning for bicycles, so to speak.

# RIGI Bici Corta
## HIGH-GRADE STEEL AND OTHER REFINEMENTS

**VARIETY**
RACING, CURIOSITY

**COUNTRY**
ITALY

**DATE**
c. 1979

**WEIGHT**
9.6 KG (21.2 LB)

**FRAME**
POLISHED STAINLESS STEEL, 55 CM (21.7 IN.) HIGH

**GEARS**
2 × 6, DERAILLEUR CAMPAGNOLO RALLY

**BRAKES**
RIM SIDE PULLCAMPAGNOLO SUPER RECORD

**TYRES**
27 IN. TUBULAR

This model bears the epithet 'Bici Corta' (short bike), and any tape measure confirms that it is 6 centimetres shorter than conventional racing bikes, with a wheelbase measuring 37.5 inches. (See the W. & R. Baines V.S. 37 on page 156.)

With the foreshortened wheelbase the seat tube needs to split for the rear wheel to sit through the middle. Just like the V.S. 37, the Rigi (short for Rinaldi Giorgio, the name of the company's founder) promises perfect manoeuvrability for time trials and superior handling on hill climbs.

The frame consists of stainless steel, drawing upon aerospace technology, with a particular silver solder required to connect the tubes. The bike was made by the Rima company (short for Rinaldi Marco, son of Giorgio), manufacturer of office equipment and furniture for educational institutions. The number of the bicycle shown is 2.

In 1979 the Rigi Bici Corta was nominated for the 'Compasso d'Oro' – an award given for excellent Italian design.

# BERMA Professional
## WHEN CHROME GETS COLOURFUL

**VARIETY**
RACING

**COUNTRY**
ITALY

**DATE**
c. 1980

**WEIGHT**
9.2 KG (20.3 LB)

**FRAME**
CHROMED STEEL + LACQUER,
57.5 CM (22.6 IN.) HIGH

**GEARS**
2 × 6 DERAILLEUR
CAMPAGNOLO SUPER RECORD ICS

**BRAKES**
RIM SIDE PULL
MODOLO PROFESSIONAL

**TYRES**
27 IN. TUBULAR

Mario Bertocco was a mechanic in the Torpado team when he founded his company, Berma. The name was a portmanteau of his surname and forename, and today his grandchildren continue to run the company and bike trade in Padua, Italy.

When the sophisticated and bestselling Professional was being produced Mario's sons, Antonio and Renzo, were at the helm. The bronze-coloured Professional was glazed, a technique that first appeared in the 1920s when Harry Wyld was racing for Selbach and his bikes attracted particular attention for their Golden Wyld glaze. The process involved painting clear varnish over nickel-plated or chrome-plated tubes, and has gone in and out of popularity as a finish over the decades.

In the era of the Berma Professional, Campagnolo's expensive Super Record groupset made with titanium parts, was already legendary. Ever since the company's founder Tullio Campagnolo had invented the quick-release axle in

1930 (see page 13), the company had been ahead of the competition in terms of innovation (and price) – with the exception of his first gear system, the Cambio Corsa model. On this bicycle, the rear wheel still had to be loosened when changing gear. In the early 1950s, however, the Gran Sport gear system saw a development that led directly (with few modifications) to the Super Record model used on the Berma Professional. It was in production until 1986.

# GAZELLE
## Champion Mondial
### THE CRUCIAL 34 MM

**VARIETY**
RACING

**COUNTRY**
NETHERLANDS

**DATE**
c. 1981

**WEIGHT**
10.2 KG (22.5 LB)

**FRAME**
VARNISHED STEEL,
60 CM (23.6 IN.) HIGH

**GEARS**
2 × 6, DERAILLEUR
CAMPAGNOLO NUOVO RECORD

**BRAKES**
RIM SIDE PULL
CAMPAGNOLO RECORD

**TYRES**
27 IN. TUBULAR

The frame construction and paint job on the Gazelle Champion Mondial road bicycle was beautiful, and resulted in a clean design that eschewed any special effects. Although the bicycle's most outstanding quality was its sensational riding experience, it became renowned for its original Colrout cranks. Described in France – its homeland of production – as being manivelles excentriques ('eccentric cranks'), the crank lever was at least 34 millimetres (1.4 inches) short of the standard. This meant that the handlebars and saddle needed to be adjusted a similar distance to achieve a comfortable seating position. Needless to say, as the Gazelle's design has evolved over the years, the manivelles excentriques have been phased out.

Gazelle road bicycles do not, perhaps, get as much recognition as they should, for they do deserve a place on the world stage. It can be no accident that Dutchman Jan Raas and the Frisol-Gazelle team had so much success in the Milan–San Remo race in 1977 on this model.

# C.B.T. ITALIA
## Champions
## A DENT FOR
## MANOEUVRABILITY

**VARIETY**
RACING

**COUNTRY**
ITALY

**DATE**
c. 1985

**WEIGHT**
9.2 KG (20.3 LB)

**FRAME**
VARNISHED STEEL, 57 CM (22.4 IN.) HIGH

**GEARS**
2 × 6, DERAILLEUR CAMPAGNOLO SUPER RECORD

**BRAKES**
RIM SIDE PULL CAMPAGNOLO SUPER RECORD

**TYRES**
27 IN. TUBULAR

The company name is an abbreviation of 'Costruzione Biciclette Tardivo', and C.B.T. Italia was founded in the mid-1950s by Giovanni Tardivo.

It was not until the mid-1970s that Giovanni's son Guido set out to include racing bikes in the programme. When his brother Bruno joined the business, racing bikes became the main focus and were even exhibited on Bruno Tardivo's ground-breaking trade show stalls.

The Champions racing bike had a split seat tube to make space for the rear wheel. The seat stays home in directly on the seat clamp bolt, and the rear seat stay bridge comes straight from the wind tunnel (or at least it looks as if it does). The PMP cranks were the result of a particularly ambitious mistake, believing that the angle in the cranks evened out the tread at the dead centres. Today it is known that this made the cranks heavier – and they have, of course, now become coveted collector's items.

C.B.T. Italia also used black chrome-plating on their bicycles but not as early as Steyr-Daimler-Puch (see page 158).

# 3RENSHO Super Record Export
## AERODYNAMICS AT ITS BEST

**VARIETY**
RACING

**COUNTRY**
JAPAN

**DATE**
c. 1984

**WEIGHT**
9.3 KG (20.5 LB)

**FRAME**
VARNISHED STEEL, 57.5 CM (22.6 IN.) HIGH

**GEARS**
2 × 7, DERAILLEUR SHIMANO DURA-ACE AX

**BRAKES**
RIM CENTRE PULL SHIMANO DURA-ACE AX

**TYRES**
27 IN. TUBULAR

Few Japanese frame builders have gained international acclaim, but Yoshi Konno is an exception. He started disassembling and re-soldering Cinelli frames after the 1964 Olympic Games in Tokyo, and began selling his exquisite, finely built bikes under the Cherubim Cyclone marque in 1973. He has subsequently created many original frame designs that have become highly desirable collectors' items. Konno named his company 3Rensho – meaning 'three victories' – and indeed riders such as Nelson Veils, Koichi Nakano, Dave Grylls and Bob Mionske have all triumphed on a Konno bicycle.

Features such as consistent aerodynamics (particularly in the head tube and upper sections of the seat stays), along with running the brake cable through the seat tube, are the technical keys keeping a Konno bike ahead of the racing pack.

The frame of the bicycle shown is number 6120.

# KIRK Precision
## LIGHT AND
## INFLAMMABLE

**VARIETY**
RACING

**COUNTRY**
UNITED KINGDOM

**DATE**
c. 1988

**WEIGHT**
10.4 KG (22.9 LB)

**FRAME**
VARNISHED MAGNESIUM,
53 CM (20.9 IN.) HIGH

**GEARS**
2 × 8, DERAILLEUR
SHIMANO DURA-ACE

**BRAKES**
RIM CENTRE PULL
WEINMANN DELTA PRO

**TYRES**
27 IN. TUBULAR

Limited First Edition

Frank Kirk

The fact that this bike shares its name with a space traveller familiar to TV audiences points to a future that has long since been overtaken by the present. The frame of the Kirk racing bike is cast from a magnesium alloy. Although magnesium is even lighter than aluminium, it is unfortunately also highly inflammable – after all, it is one of the most reactive metals – bringing corrosion into the equation.

Because the frame is cast (and so not hollow like tubes), the weight advantage is also lost. The fact that the Kirk was very prone to warping and was only available in one or two frame heights also diminished its success. Frank Kirk first presented his invention at the New York Cycle Show in May 1986, but he concealed the fact that the exhibits had frames composed of aluminium. The volume of orders placed was high, and indeed proved slightly embarrassing as they were a struggle to fulfil. When the new factory was finally finished, it sadly burned down a few days after production started – the result of magnesium dust in the air spontaneously combusting. For any Kirk Precisions that actually made it to the customer, the bicycle's shift lever mount or the seat stay bridge would sometimes break. With this unhappy record, the Kirk Precision (number 1426 shown here) makes a perfect show-piece of imperfect design.

# EDDY MERCKX
## Corsa Extra
### FROM THE MASTER HIMSELF

**VARIETY**
RACING

**COUNTRY**
BELGIUM

**DATE**
1990

**WEIGHT**
10.2 KG (22.5 LB)

**FRAME**
VARNISHED STEEL,
58.5 CM (23 IN.) HIGH

**GEARS**
2 × 7, DERAILLEUR
CAMPAGNOLO C RECORD

**BRAKES**
RIM CENTRE PULL
CAMPAGNOLO C RECORD DELTA

**TYRES**
27 IN. TUBULAR

When active on the racing circuit Eddy Merckx rode
bikes that bore his name, but they were produced
by Faliero Masi, Ernesto Colnago, Ugo de Rosa or the
Belgian firm Kessels. It was not until 1980 that Merckx
started his own company, after Ugo de Rosa had told
him the secrets of frame building.

In 1990 Merckx celebrated his tenth anniversary
by creating a special edition model. The bicycle here
is number H7XC6915. It was painted in the colours of
the Molteni team and named after a sausage-making
dynasty from Milan who sponsored the professional
racing team from 1958 through to 1976. The most
successful rider in this team was Merckx himself. Of
the 633 victories taken by the Molteni team, he had
won 246, even on the early Merckx racing bikes.

The company still exists, and Eddy Merckx
probably remains the most successful racing cyclist
of all time even today. No one else has been able to
realize such broad and varied achievements, and as
a result that era of racing was marked by his victories.

For many fans the 1970s were the heyday of cycle
racing – and also of racing bike building.

# 'Messenger Bike'
## USING THE ROAD
## AS A RACING TRACK

**VARIETY**
SINGLESPEED, URBAN

**COUNTRY**
ITALY

**DATE**
c. 1978

**WEIGHT**
8 KG (17.6 LB)

**FRAME**
VARNISHED STEEL,
56 CM (22 IN.) HIGH

**GEAR**
1, FIXED

**TYRES**
27 IN. TUBULAR

The 'Messenger Bike' would have suited modern cycle couriers as it was the ultimate track bicycle with fixed wheels. The frame is probably from Italy where, at the time of its creation in the late 1970s, nobody could have suspected that many years later the design would ride a fashion wave leading to its widespread rediscovery.

In order to brake without brakes, the upper body needed to be shifted forwards over the handlebars and the rear wheel stopped using the cranks.

Using this method, the rider skidded to a stop. The bracing spokes on the front wheel offered better aerodynamics, while the bridge (designed in the Gothic style) sitting between the seat stays is a delight even when stationary. The high quality Dura-Ace-10 components of the 'Messenger Bike' (see also the Inbike/Textima on page 78) have been judged by NJS (Nihon Jitensha Shinkokai), the Japanese Keirin authority, to be suitable for their powerful track cyclists.

# MERCIAN 'Custom'
## SPECIALISTS ON THE ROAD

**VARIETY**
URBAN, SINGLESPEED

**COUNTRY**
UNITED KINGDOM

**DATE**
2005

**WEIGHT**
8.5 KG (18.7 LB)

**FRAME**
VARNISHED STEEL,
58.7 CM (23.1 IN.) HIGH

**GEAR**
1, FIXED

**TYRES**
28 IN. WIRED

The fact that the left-hand chain stay of this Mercian is chrome-plated – instead of the right one as would generally be expected – causes great interest, and is the decision of the first frame owner. The Mercian was handcrafted according to his specifications over a period of nine months. The bicycle shown here is number 2008/6.

The fork is straight in the manner of polo bikes, but the latter are ridden with free-wheeling and braking to enable good speed of manoeuvrability. The Mercian can only travel along mainly straight lines as, due to the short wheelbase, the front tyre collides with the pedals when cornering. And because of the fixed wheel, the pedals continue to move relentlessly as long as the bicycle is moving.

Mercian bicycles have been produced in Derby, England, since 1946. Despite relocating several times, the manufacturer has never left the city.

The enthusiasm for Mercian bikes has been constant, and in 2007 Mercian teamed up with the fashion designer Paul Smith (see foreword, page 6) to produce two special-edition models. These, of course, were given particularly tasteful paintwork.

# GT Vengeance
# Aero Mark Allen
## THE TRIATHLETE'S
## BEST FRIEND

**VARIETY**
RACING

**COUNTRY**
USA

**DATE**
1998

**WEIGHT**
9.3 KG (20.5 LB)

**FRAME**
VARNISHED ALUMINIUM, 'LARGE' HEIGHT

**GEARS**
2 × 8, DERAILLEUR SHIMANO 600

**BRAKES**
RIM SIDE PULL SHIMANO 600

**TYRES**
26 IN. TUBULAR

To achieve perfect aerodynamics for the GT Vengeance, even the teardrop shape was reinvented and lengthened until it bore a subtle resemblance to the blade of a knife. This is how you might imagine the cross-section of most of the tubes on this GT triathlon frame. It was developed for the US Olympic team competing in the 1996 Atlanta Games, and was also featured in the normal GT sales programme, accumulating an impressive record of success both there and elsewhere.

The shape achieved more success with Mark Allen, the man who was winning virtually every triathlon around 1990. He was one of the Big Four of the sport, voted 'Triathlete of the Year' six times by Triathlete magazine and named 'World's Fittest Man' in 1997 by Outside magazine. In the same year the GT Vengeance Mark Allen Edition arrived at GT dealerships with 26-inch wheels, three frame heights and lovingly executed details. Instead of a conventional seat clamp, for instance, there are three recessed wormscrews that secure the seatpost (which is, of course, also aerodynamic in cross-section). The bicycle featured here is number 229.

GT was founded in 1979 by Gary Turner and his friend Richard Long in Santa Ana, California, and they soon expanded their range of BMX bikes to include mountain bikes and, eventually, racing bikes. The fact that virtually nobody outside the cycling community took any notice when the business went bust on 11 September 2001 is understandable; the world's attention was elsewhere that day.

# AIRNIMAL
## Chameleon
### THE BEST OF
### TWO WORLDS

**VARIETY**
FOLDING, RACING

**COUNTRY**
UNITED KINGDOM

**DATE**
c. 2005

**WEIGHT**
10 KG (22 LB)

**FRAME**
VARNISHED ALUMINIUM,
49.4 CM (19.4 IN.) HIGH

**GEARS**
3 × 9, DERAILLEUR SHIMANO 105

**BRAKES**
RIM SIDE PULL SHIMANO 105

**TYRES**
24 IN. WIRED

The British company Airnimal had similar ambitions to those of (virtually) all folding bike manufacturers: to produce a bike that was small when folded but gave a big performance on the road. The Airnimal Chameleon, which was rolled out onto the streets after four years of development, rests on unusual 24-inch wheels. In fact it rides like a high-end, light bike – which is what it is, of course.

The Chameleon's rear-wheel suspension uses an elastomer to take the edge off any bumps in the road surface, supposedly without swallowing up any of the pedalling power in the process. However, the rear swinging fork actually folds away under the frame when the bike is folded. Anyone prepared to invest a few minutes using a tool can walk away with a very small, more compacted package, but anyone wanting to spend only a few seconds folding the bike without a tool has a rather larger package to carry, which seems a fair compromise.

The Airnimal Chameleon has already proved several times how well it performs on the road in competitive events. It successfully took part in the classic Paris–Brest–Paris race, for example, and British rider Peter Howard won a bronze medal in a Senior's Triathlon World Championship race in New Zealand on a Chameleon.

# DAHON
# Hammerhead 5.0
## A BIKE IN
## TWO MILLION

**VARIETY**
CURIOSITY, RACING

**COUNTRY**
TAIWAN/USA

**DATE**
c. 2005

**WEIGHT**
8.9 KG (19.6 LB)

**FRAME**
VARNISHED ALUMINIUM,
50.5 CM (19.9 IN.) HIGH

**GEARS**
10, DERAILLEUR
SHIMANO DURA-ACE (REAR)

**BRAKES**
RIM SIDE PULL

**TYRES**
20 IN. WIRED

Dr David Hon moved to California from Hong Kong to study physics, and it was there that he got to know and love bikes. Together with his brother Henry he studied every existing folding bike patent and showcased his first prototype at the New York Bike Show in 1980.

Hon was able to get hold of investment in order to manufacture, and so in 1982 he founded his bicycle company, Dahon. Since then his company has sold more than two million bikes, including some that cannot be folded such as the Dahon Hammerhead.

Even without any folding technology, the bike impresses with its extremely compact frame in dual arc design and with Kinetix Q suspension. Thanks to the aluminium tubes, the Hammerhead weighs only 10.2 kilograms (22.5 lb), while the tuned 5.0 model featured here weighs a mere 8.9 kilograms (19.6 lb).

As a result, Dahon invites categorization as a 'mini' bicycle; however, this can have wrong connotations. The handling is brilliant and very mature, and the Hammerhead thus sits perfectly within the tradition of the Alex Moulton bicycles (see pages 100 and 102), when their creator Alex Moulton ushered in a new era of bicycle construction in the 1960s.

The impression of top quality in riding this Hammerhead (number D512705410) is supported by the exquisite 20-inch HED wheels, handcrafted like all of the firm's 16-inch wheel models. Only the garage where HED began in the 1980s has since been replaced by larger premises.

# BIKE FRIDAY
# New World Tourist
## SMALL WHEELS, BIG TRIP

**VARIETY**
FOLDING, RACING, TOURING

**COUNTRY**
USA

**DATE**
1998

**WEIGHT**
10 KG (22 LB)

**FRAME**
VARNISHED STEEL,
58 CM (22.8 IN.) HIGH

**GEARS**
3 × 8, DERAILLEUR CAMPAGNOLO (REAR I),
HUB GEAR SRAM (REAR II)

**BRAKES**
RIM V-BRAKE AVID

**TYRES**
20 IN. WIRED

206

Bike Friday is not about taking your bike out of the car boot to ride short distances – its aim is rather to escape into the wider world. Alan and Hanz Scholz initially experimented with tandems, but their friend Richard Gabriel inspired them to build touring bicycles that could also be transported inconspicuously on other forms of transport.

The diamond framed 'World Tourist' and its successor, the 'New World Tourist' (number 3778 shown here) with its stable central tube, have an intelligent folding mechanism. Due to angled hinges

the bicycle's parts avoid one another as it folds, and when completely folded up the entire bicycle will fit into a suitcase that can be taken on trains and aeroplanes without any problems.

When you are riding the Bike Friday the suitcase can be towed as a trailer, filled with all your luggage, and thanks to the Sachs/SRAM-3x8 components, there are plenty of speeds available. Alan and Hanz Scholz particularly like the idea of seeing people riding the Bike Friday away from the airport directly after landing in their destination country.

# SKOOT INTERNATIONAL
# LTD Skoot
## TO HAVE
## AND TO HOLD

**VARIETY**
CURIOSITY, FOLDING, URBAN

**COUNTRY**
UNITED KINGDOM

**DATE**
2001

**WEIGHT**
14.5 KG (32 LB)

**FRAME**
PLASTIC + STEEL,
53 CM (20.9 IN.) HIGH

**GEARS**
1

**BRAKES**
RIM SIDE PULL

**TYRES**
12 IN. WIRED

however, it passes so convincingly as a piece of luggage that you don't need to buy a bicycle ticket for it.

Designer Vincent Fallon and his son Vaughan founded the Skoot International company in Colchester, UK, to produce this bicycle. However, the Lustran plastic for the suitcase-shaped frame (also used for car dashboards and bumpers on account of its robustness) and the mudguards is produced by Bayer, the company based in Leverkusen in Germany.

This might look like a joke, but it is a serious product – a suitcase in the form of a bike, and vice versa. When the seat, wheels and handlebars are pulled out and the cranks attached, the Skoot can go a short distance (watched by amused passers-by). There is even room to carry a briefcase or laptop in the suitcase while riding.

Carrying the bicycle stowed away in the suitcase over long distances is not really an option, as the Skoot weighs 14.5 kilograms (32 lb). On public transport,

# T&C
# Pocket Bici
## FOLD UP AND AWAY

**VARIETY**
CURIOSITY, FOLDING

**COUNTRY**
ITALY

**DATE**
c. 1963

**WEIGHT**
15.4 KG (34 LB)

**FRAME**
VARNISHED STEEL,
37 CM (13 IN.) HIGH

**GEAR**
1

**BRAKES**
RIM SIDE PULL

**TYRES**
12 IN. WIRED

When folded the T&C Pocket Bici resembles a
sculpture in honour of entropy – so it may be simplest
to keep it stowed away in its special carrying case or
in a suitcase. Even when ready to ride, the design is
distinctive and causes a sensation in the cycle lanes.

The Pocket Bici was invented and patented by T&C
(Tresoldi & Casiraghi SRL) in Carugate in the province
of Milan. They sold approximately 2,500 of them,
mostly in China, but the response from cyclists in their
home country was rather more modest.

The folding mechanism is rather complex in the
way it functions, and the handling is as you would
expect from a folding bike with 12-inch tyres – rather
prone to twisting. Nonetheless, the cable brakes
suggest grown-up ambitions. The dual transmission
seems particularly extravagant – without it, the front
chain ring would surely be bigger than the wheels.

# KATAKURA Silk
## Porta Cycle
### THE JAPANESE ART
### OF FOLDING

**VARIETY**
FOLDING, URBAN

**COUNTRY**
JAPAN

**DATE**
c. 1964

**WEIGHT**
16.4 KG (36.2 LB)

**FRAME**
VARNISHED STEEL,
33 CM (13 IN.) HIGH

**GEAR**
1

**BRAKES**
RIM SIDE PULL JS (FRONT),
COASTER BRAKE (REAR)

**TYRES**
20 IN. WIRED

214

In the mid-1960s Japan looked a great deal to Europe for inspiration, and this was particularly true when it came to design. Both folding bikes and rockets were very hip at the time, as is evident from this Japanese example. The rocket-like design can be seen on the underside of the handlebars, the two halves of which can be folded in the same way as the right-hand foot crank.

This bicycle was not developed to ease space problems in Japanese cities and in the boots of small cars. It was initially developed to support the supplies for Vietnamese troops in the Vietnam War. Only after the conflict did it begin its civilian career – for example, in the mid-1960s in Germany where, like most folding bikes, it was marketed as a car-bicycle. Only a few folding bikes had full-sized wheels, such as the René Herse Demontable (see page 40), the BSA Paratrooper (see page 218) or Trussardi (see page 122).

Katakura, which ceased manufacturing in the 1990s, operated mainly as a silk-spinning company, but its portfolio also stretched to racing bikes.

Incidentally, anyone who catches a glimpse of a folded Katakura Silk Porta Cycle will appreciate how popular yoga must be.

# LE PETIT BI
## WHERE FOLDING
## BEGAN

**VARIETY**
FOLDING, URBAN

**COUNTRY**
FRANCE

**DATE**
c. 1937

**WEIGHT**
15.1 KG (33.3 LB)

**FRAME**
VARNISHED STEEL,
26.5 CM (10.4 IN.) HIGH

**GEARS**
3, DERAILLEUR SIMPLEX TOURISTE (REAR)

**BRAKES**
RIM SIDE PULL DAUNAY

**TYRES**
18 IN. WIRED

The parallels between Le Petit Bi and the Katakura Silk Porta Cycle (page 214) are uncanny, especially when it comes to the folding mechanism of the handlebars.

Le Petit Bi was possibly even the first bicycle with small wheels which could be folded and was designed for adults. The frame was untouched by the folding mechanism, however, meaning that the amount of space saved was rather limited. The bike nonetheless became shorter and lower, and could even be rested upright on its ample pannier rack – although it was advisable to remove the saddlebags first.

Noteworthy features were the brakes, the leather seat, which was ornately decorated with embossed detail, and the sprung seatpost – an everyday feature today, but a novelty in the late 1930s.

The handlebars pre-empted the high-riser trend of the 1970s, but the credit for sparking the fashion for bikes with small wheels must be claimed by Alex Moulton (see the Speedsix on page 102).

# BSA
# Paratrooper
## A BICYCLE
## FROM THIN AIR

**VARIETY**
CURIOSITY, FOLDING

**COUNTRY**
UNITED KINGDOM

**DATE**
c. 1940

**WEIGHT**
13.6 KG (30 LB)

**FRAME**
VARNISHED STEEL,
44 CM (17.3 IN.) HIGH

**GEAR**
1

**BRAKES**
RIM CENTRE PULL

**TYRES**
26 IN. WIRED

This paratrooper bike by BSA was dropped by the British military in World War II with its own parachute fastened to the wheels. There were more than 60,000 produced on the British army's orders, and specialist trainers were employed to advise troops on using the bike, especially on first landing. The paratrooper bike featured in the D-Day landings, taking its part in history.

The seat and handlebars pointed downwards, and they had to be pulled out as far as possible and only loosely fastened. On impact with the ground, the seat would be pushed into the seat tube and the handlebars pushed into the steering tube, helping to lessen the force of the impact.

Although this folding bike was quite a weight, it would have hung from the parachute even more awkwardly without a folding frame. A smaller bike would also have been easier to drop through the air, but on the ground it would have been far less suitable for the terrain.

The pedals could be pushed through the cranks, which ensured a smaller overall package size when fully folded.

BSA stands for 'Birmingham Small Arms', which bridged the gap perfectly with the rest of the firm's products. In 1983 the fashion company Trussardi adopted the BSA Paratrooper bicycle and turned it into a high-end touring bike with all sorts of leather appliqué (see page 122).

# 'Inconnu'
# THE HANDYMAN'S
# FRIEND

**VARIETY**
CURIOSITY, FOLDING, URBAN

**COUNTRY**
FRANCE

**DATE**
c. 1950

**WEIGHT**
14.5 KG (32 LB)

**FRAME**
VARNISHED STEEL,
32 CM (12.6 IN.) HIGH

**GEAR**
1

**BRAKES REAR**
RIM SIDE PULL CLB 650

**TYRES**
14 IN. WIRED

Anyone wanting to use this folding bike for cycling needs to plan their daily schedule carefully. The design arouses a sense of foreboding on first glance, and this is confirmed in practice. It takes around an hour to fold this bicycle and unfold it again, when you are not familiar with its ways. When folded, it is even more cumbersome, being now flatter and broader, and must be towed like a trailer – and that's exactly what it's made for. This bike is a trailer for towing collapsible boats on land, for example when weirs of mills or power stations interrupt the riverbed. The boat itself then rests on the rubber covers of the tubes. When the boat is in the water, the bike is stowed away on the afterdeck. The lack of a second brake also indicates that the bike is not really made for cycling.

A noteworthy feature of the 'Inconnu' (Unknown) is the bracket for the rear brake, which is welded on. Such details help to explain the bicycle's weight of 14.5 kilograms (32 lb). Perhaps due to its many design faults, both designer and manufacturer prefer to remain anonymous. No clues are found anywhere on the bike featured, although this may also be due to the patinated paintwork. There is only one 'Inconnu' bicycle known – and this is it.

# DUEMILA Duemila
## POP TO THE SHOPS ON A ROCKET DESIGN

**VARIETY**
CURIOSITY, FOLDING, URBAN

**COUNTRY**
ITALY

**DATE**
c. 1968

**WEIGHT**
19.5 KG (43 LB)

**FRAME**
VARNISHED STEEL, ADJUSTABLE HEIGHT

**GEAR**
1

**BRAKES**
RIM SIDE PULL (FRONT), COASTER BRAKE (REAR)

**TYRES**
20 IN. WIRED

The bicycle's name alone (meaning 'two thousand') pointed towards the future and neatly reflected the obsession with space travel prevalent in the late 1960s.

Duemila's logo continued the theme, depicting the brand name as the atomic nucleus, circled by electrons. At the time, it was a forward-looking design, but today, just like the Bohr model of atomic attraction, the design is out of date. In its era, the Duemila turned a quick trip to the shops into a mission to the final frontier with its rocket-like design.

The Duemila was one of the most beautiful folding bikes of a classic era – and, interestingly, one of the most impractical. The height of the saddle, for instance, could not be adjusted in the usual fashion by extending the seat tube; only by tilting it you could gain or lose a few precious centimetres.

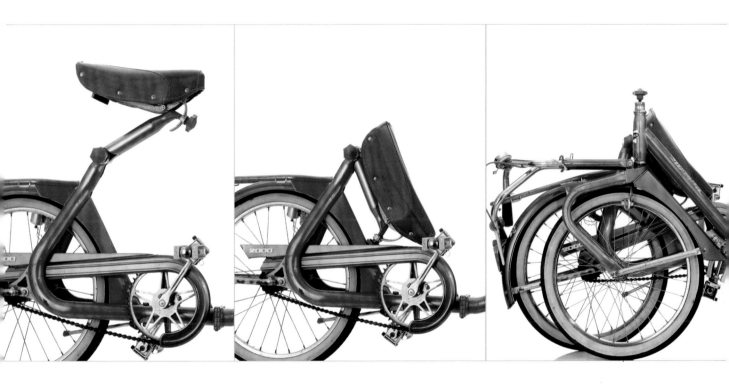

# BICKERTON
## Portable
## A WHIFF OF ROLLS ROYCE

**VARIETY**
FOLDING, URBAN

**COUNTRY**
UNITED KINGDOM

**DATE**
c. 1971

**WEIGHT**
9.6 KG (21.2 LB)

**FRAME**
ALUMINIUM, 26 CM (10.2 IN.) HIGH

**GEARS**
3, HUB GEAR STURMEY ARCHER (REAR)

**BRAKES**
RIM SIDE PULL WEINMANN TYPE 730

**TYRES**
14 IN. WIRED (FRONT),
16 IN. WIRED (REAR)

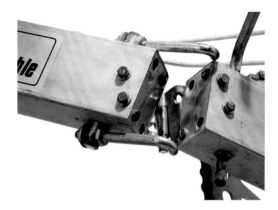

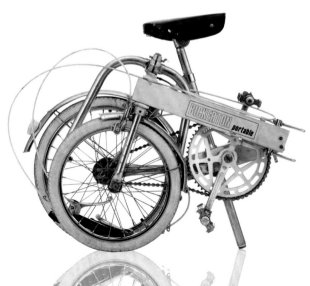

This was a bike built by a Rolls Royce aerospace engineer who, despite having lost his driving licence, still wanted to travel in style with a mode of transport that matched his social status. The Bickerton Portable was the first truly lightweight, easy to carry folding bicycle. It folded up so small that it even fitted in the boot of a classic Mini. It had a fully aluminium frame and parts – steel rims proving the only exception.

From the safe distance of a few decades, it can be said that the Bickerton Portable does have some design faults – not quite the equal of a Rolls Royce for prestige and solidity. It is extremely prone to twisting, frequently throwing its riders over the soft handlebars. After even its designer, Harry Bickerton, had a fall, he wrote in a brochure: 'Designed for intelligent competent human beings, not gorillas.'

Sales of the Bickerton were excellent, however, and from 1971 to 1989 around 50,000 were made. The bicycle shown here is number A2033.

# STRIDA LTD
## Strida 1
### BEST IN SHOW

**VARIETY**
CURIOSITY, FOLDING, URBAN

**COUNTRY**
UNITED KINGDOM

**DATE**
1988

**WEIGHT**
11 KG (24.3 LB)

**FRAME**
POWDER-COATED ALUMINIUM,
ADJUSTABLE HEIGHT

**GEAR**
1

**BRAKES**
DRUM BRAKE

**TYRES**
16 IN. WIRED

The Strida 1, designed by Mark Sanders, gained numerous accolades at its première in Britain in 1987. It received Best New Machine, Best British Product and Best in Show at the UK Cyclex Bicycle Innovation Awards in 1988. A commercial success from its conception, the Strida 1 series remains in production today.

The bicycle was designed for distances of up to 6 kilometres (4.7 miles) and, with its small wheels and upright commuting position, it is not comfortable to ride much further.

Technical highlights of the Strida 1 include the toothed belt drive, cable pulls laid in aluminium tubes, innovative plastic wheels with integrated side reflectors, and wheels fixed to the frame on one side only. Moreover, it takes only around ten seconds to fold up.

The Strida is manufactured in Taiwan, where the fifth-generation Strida is now being produced.

# ELETTROMONTAGGI
# SRL Zoombike
## THE COMMUTERS'
## CYCLE-STICK

**VARIETY**
CURIOSITY, FOLDING

**COUNTRY**
ITALY/GERMANY

**DATE**
c. 1994

**WEIGHT**
10.3 KG (22.7 LB)

**FRAME**
ALUMINIUM,
55 CM (21.7 IN.) HIGH

**GEARS**
3, DERAILLEUR (REAR)

**BRAKES**
RIM SIDE PULL EXAGE

**TYRES**
14 IN. WIRED

The original intention of designer Richard Sapper (designer for Alessi, Artemide, Mercedes-Benz and more) was to create a bicycle to aid the mobility of city dwellers, to be used in conjunction with public transport. After ten years in development, the Elettromontaggi SRL Zoombike was launched in 1998 at the Frankfurt Auto Salon, marketed as the vehicle of choice for covering large distances at the fair. Although popular, and despite the 60 prototypes made, the bicycle failed to make it into series production.

The Zoombike boasted a lightweight aluminium frame and a linear, clean form with perfectly integrated parts. When folded, the triple-gear derailleur sat neatly in the central tube along with a headlamp and battery; a cleverly placed LED in the top tube served as the rear light, and the internal Bowden cables bent with the frame. When folded, the Zoombike bore a resemblance to a folded Strida 1 (see page 228).

# SACHS Tango
## A HEAVYWEIGHT BEFORE ITS DEMISE

**VARIETY**
FOLDING, URBAN

**COUNTRY**
NETHERLANDS

**DATE**
2000

**WEIGHT**
20.6 KG (45.4 LB)

**FRAME**
PLASTIC-COATED ALUMINIUM
+ STEEL, 53 CM (20.9 IN.) HIGH

**GEARS**
4, BRACKET GEAR SHIMANO NEXUS (REAR)

**BRAKES**
DRUM BRAKE SHIMANO

**TYRES**
16 IN. WIRED

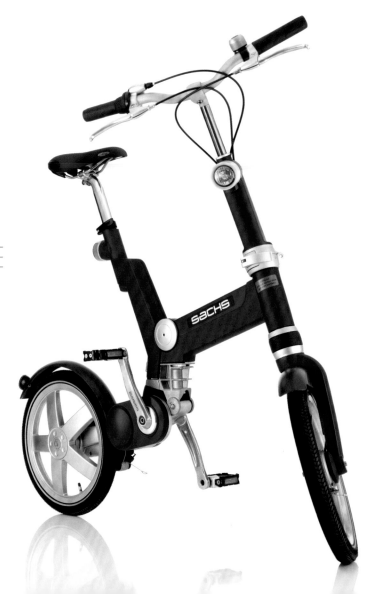

The Tango folding bicycle might appear German at first glance, but its origins lie in the Netherlands. Designed by Urban Solutions, a Dutch design firm that specialized in city cars, the Tango 'Car Bike' shares many similarities with its larger, 4-wheeled cousins. For example, wires and Bowden cables are laid in the bodywork, making the bicycle low-maintenance, and it also boasts full suspension.

The Tango first appeared in 1997 at the Vision 2000 design competition organized by Shimano. It was an instant winner, beating 12 other competitors. Sadly, it did not prove a commercial success in the long term, and even small series production could not prevent Urban Solutions from going bankrupt.

Resurrection came through Sachs, a German-based motorcycle manufacturer, which marketed the Tango as the perfect partner to a car. Sachs promoted its qualities – a polyurethane coating (making it low-maintenance and washable) and a full suspension with rubber buffers – but the high retail price and weight continued to affect sales.

Even when car manufacturer VW took on production it was not successful. The Tango seemed to be doomed, and eventually it faded quietly away.

# RIESE & MÜLLER
## Birdy 10th
HAPPY BIRTHDAY TO ME

**VARIETY**
FOLDING, RACING

**COUNTRY**
GERMANY

**DATE**
2005

**WEIGHT**
10.9 KG (24 LB)

**FRAME**
ALUMINIUM,
36 CM (14.2 IN.) HIGH

**GEARS**
2 × 9,
DERAILLEUR SHIMANO 105

**BRAKES**
RIM SIDE PULL
TEKTRO RXS

**TYRES**
20 IN. WIRED

Markus Riese and Heiko Müller, the creators of the Birdy 10th, claim that this bicycle is a legend and that it rides like a big bike. Even those not interested in the former claim might care about the latter, particularly in the case of the 10th anniversary model.

With 20-inch tyres, Birdy 10th rolls over obstacles with a little more confidence than the other models with their smaller, 18-inch wheels. The special anniversary series was limited to 100 pieces. You could choose between straight handlebars or drop bars, but Shimano-105 racing bike components came as standard.

Birdy bicycles have been around since 1995. These modifications were noticeable for the first time on the model shown here (number PG05120445), although Birdy's had received several improvements in the previous decade.

This clever move subtly won the affections of their fans. Riese and Müller had great success with Japan in particular, a feat that had only been achieved by Brompton Titanium S2L-X (see page 236).

Birdy, incidentally, got a new design range in 2006, and immediately won the iF Product Design Award.

# BROMPTON
## Titanium S2L-X
### FASTER, SMALLER AND MORE INGENIOUS

**VARIETY**
FOLDING, URBAN

**COUNTRY**
UNITED KINGDOM

**DATE**
2009

**WEIGHT**
8.9 KG (19.6 LB)

**FRAME**
VARNISHED STEEL + TITANIUM,
23.8 CM (9.4 IN.) HIGH

**GEARS**
2, DERAILLEUR BROMPTON (REAR)

**BRAKES**
RIM SIDE PULL BROMPTON

**TYRES**
16 IN. WIRED

When it comes to the rankings of top folding bikes, the Brompton is in the premier league. It seems virtually impossible for a bicycle to fold any faster smaller or more ingeniously; Brompton does, after all, have over 30 years of experience in folding bicycles.

In 1976 Andrew Ritchley was inspired by the Bickerton Portable (see page 226), but he wanted to implement the idea more effectively. The patent specification shows a cross between the Bickerton and Le Petit Bi (see page 216). Another ten years passed before the first Brompton series model was produced, and then the story of its success began.

The Brompton mainly appealed to people travelling in cities and beyond who had discovered the joy of using a folding bike to complement other forms of transport.

Owing to its titanium rear swinging fork, seatpost and fork, the Brompton S2L-X is also the lightweight model of the catalogue. Along with a few tuning components (cranks, handlebars, seat and pedals), the example featured (number 271515/PS6102) weighs a mere 8.9 kilograms (19.6 lb). Once folded its size is 22.2 × 21.5 × 9.8 inches (56.5 × 54.5 × 25 cm) and its two-speed gear system makes it ideal for the city.

Brompton bikes are designed and produced in London and then exported throughout the world – in particularly small boxes, of course.

# PACIFIC CYCLES
## iF Mode
ANSWERING A
MODERN NEED

**VARIETY**
FOLDING, URBAN

**COUNTRY**
TAIWAN

**DATE**
2009

**WEIGHT**
14.7 KG (32.4 LB)

**FRAME**
VARNISHED ALUMINIUM,
33 CM (13 IN.) HIGH

**GEARS**
2, BRACKET GEAR (REAR)

**BRAKES**
DISC BRAKE WINZIP

**TYRES**
26 IN. WIRED

The idea that a folding bike, together with bus, tram, underground and taxi, offers the ideal mix for urban mobility is carried forward into the modern era by the iF Mode.

Mark Sanders (also responsible for the Strida Ltd Strida I, see page 228) showcased this design at the bike fair in Taipei in 2008, and it was launched as a shaft-driven bike. The shaft drive did not work well with the bottom bracket and its 2-speed gears, which were shifted with the heel. As a result a standard chain (fully encased to protect it from bad weather) now takes care of the drive.

Despite the chain, the iF Mode cannot be called an ordinary design. The swinging arms give it a futuristic feel, and the full-size 26-inch wheels sit next to one another once the bike is folded. Both in its folded and unfolded forms, the bike resembles something from the future, so much so that 20 iF Modes even play supporting roles in the German romantic film The Days to Come, set in 2020.

Incidentally the letters 'iF' in this bicycle's name stand for Integrated Folding, and bear no relation to the iF Product Design Award (where iF stands for International Forum Design). In a neat link, however, the iF Mode bicycle did win this award in 2009, while the year before that it took the Eurobike Award.

# MFA 'LAMBRETTA'
## LIKE THE GROWN-UPS

**VARIETY**
KIDS

**COUNTRY**
FRANCE

**DATE**
c. 1960

**WEIGHT**
10.3 KG (22.7 LB)

**FRAME**
VARNISHED STEEL,
26 CM (10.2 IN.) HIGH

**GEAR**
1, FIXED

**TYRES**
12 IN. SOLID

Like the grown-ups, if the big, wide world wants to engage with children, then sometimes it has to make itself smaller-scale. This bike disguised as a motor scooter was the perfect 'vehicle' to catch a child's imagination. The MFA scooter bicycle was for children whose aspirations were greater than their sense of balance.

Although the scooter-bike had MFA (Manufacture Française d'Ameublement – a company producing various toys for children) written on the front, it was surely nicknamed something more obvious by its young riders, from 'Lambretta' to 'Vespa'. Whatever the name given to the MFA scooter-bike, it was the only bicycle on which it was appropriate to make engine noises while riding.

With this nod to the world of adults, the figure featured on the front mudguard was another nice touch. It is from the company Biemme and was sold as an original 1960s mascot for a Vespa or Lambretta.

# DUSIKA Dusika
## THE SCOOTER THAT GROWS WITH ITS OWNER

**VARIETY**
CURIOSITY, KIDS

**COUNTRY**
AUSTRIA

**DATE**
c. 1960

**WEIGHT**
10.5 KG (23.1 LB)

**FRAME**
VARNISHED STEEL,
39 CM (15.4 IN.) HIGH

**GEAR**
1

**BRAKES**
TYRE BRAKE (FRONT),
COASTER BRAKE (REAR)

**TYRES**
12 IN. WIRED

The Dusika bicycle was designed to grow alongside its young owner. It could be ridden as a self-propelled scooter by small children, and later, as the child's sense of balance improved, retooled into a more grown-up bicycle.

The seat tube, seat, cranks and seat stays are all mounted to the frame as a single unit, with the chain generating the traction. The bicycle is then ready to ride. Naturally, it can also be fitted with stabilizer wheels.

The flexible Dusika scooter bicycle could have been the ideal gift for children to relieve pressure on parents' bank accounts. However, the scooter and retro-fit pedalling unit were actually so expensive that it often proved cheaper to purchase a basic scooter followed by a separate bicycle years later.

# CARNIELLI Graziella Leopard Tipo Cross
## ENDURO WITHOUT AN ENGINE

**VARIETY**
KIDS

**COUNTRY**
ITALY

**DATE**
c. 1976

**WEIGHT**
19.5 KG (43 LB)

**FRAME**
VARNISHED STEEL,
39 CM (15.4 IN.) HIGH

**GEARS**
3, DERAILLEUR
HURET (REAR)

**BRAKES**
DRUM BRAKE

**TYRES**
20 IN. WIRED

Known as 'choppers', 'high-risers' or 'bonanza' bicycles, these were the coolest vehicle for style-loving adolescents in the late 1970s. The manufacturers retained control of their market by building only models of a small size – and so preventing the bikes from being adopted by boring adults.

Even more than MFA's 'Lambretta' scooter bicycle (page 240), Carnielli's Leopard Tipo Cross whetted a young rider's appetite for motorbikes (the bike shown here is number 552152).

Looking deceptively similar to a dirt bike (except for the banana seat), the Tipo Cross had front and rear suspension – a rarity among 1970s high-risers.

The Schwinn Orange Krate or Apple Krate began the trend for these bicycles. They had come from the USA along with the film Easy Rider, and the Raleigh Chopper from the UK rode the same wave. By this time the Carnielli company, founded in 1908, had more than 60 years' experience in manufacturing bicycles and other fitness equipment. They quickly launched the Leopard Tipo Cross.

In contrast to other bicycles such as the Chopper, the feature of the Leopard Tipo Cross that really prepared Carnielli riders for serious cycling was its weight of 19.5 kilograms (43 lb). No racing bicycle is so effective a trainer in adulthood.

# CYCLES GITANE
## 'Enfant' &
## Profil Aero TT
### LIKE FATHER
### LIKE SON

CYCLES GITANE 'ENFANT' (KIDS'; OPPOSITE)

**VARIETY**
KIDS, RACING

**COUNTRY**
FRANCE

**DATE**
1982

**WEIGHT**
9.6 KG (21.2 LB)

**FRAME**
VARNISHED STEEL,
39.2 CM (15.4 IN.) HIGH

**GEARS**
3, DERAILLEUR HURET (REAR)

**BRAKES**
RIM SIDE PULL WEINMANN TYPE 730

**TYRES**
20 IN. TUBULAR

CYCLES GITANE PROFIL AERO TT

**VARIETY**
RACING

**COUNTRY**
FRANCE

**DATE**
1981

**WEIGHT**
9.3 KG (20.5 LB)

**FRAME**
VARNISHED STEEL,
58 CM (22.8 IN.) HIGH

**GEARS**
2 × 6, DERAILLEUR SHIMANO DURA-ACE

**BRAKES**
RIM SIDE PULL SHIMANO DURA-ACE

**TYRES**
27 IN. TUBULAR

Cycles Gitane was founded by Marcel Bruneliere in 1925 in Machecoul, France, although the company's final name was not confirmed until 1930. Only in the late 1950s and early 1960s did Gitane become immortalized.

Jacques Anquetil took three of his five victories in the Tour de France on Gitanes. Since 1976 Gitane has been part of Renault, with Bernard Hinault, Laurent Fignon and Greg LeMond, among others, claiming a permanent place in the company's annals. Sadly, in 2003, Gitane sponsored a racing team for the last time.

Back in the 1970s Bernard Hinault and Gitane were experimenting with exceptionally aerodynamic time trial bikes. Years later the results were implemented in road-racing bikes.

Only the top tube is round on the Gitane Profil Aero TT featured here (number 6229081). All other tubes are drop-shaped in cross-section, the most aerodynamic shape possible. The bicycle never achieves its drag coefficient of 0.04, simply because, ironically, there is always a rider on it when it is moving. Another criticism has been levelled at the child's version (number 82056 shown here) – that it does not look like a child's bike, but a shrunken, smaller-scale version of a racing bike. Which is, of course – with all the expensive components that implies – exactly what it is.

# CINELLI
## Laser
### STEEL WIND

**VARIETY**
RACING

**COUNTRY**
ITALY

**DATE**
c. 1985

**WEIGHT**
9.5 KG (20.9 LB)

**FRAME**
VARNISHED STEEL,
55 CM (21.7 IN.) HIGH

**GEARS**
2 × 7, DERAILLEUR
CAMPAGNOLO C RECORD

**BRAKES**
RIM SIDE PULL
CAMPAGNOLO SUPER RECORD

**TYRES**
27 IN. TUBULAR

If ever anyone had to choose a single bicycle model to illustrate the new aerodynamics wave, the Cinelli Laser would represent this era. It marked the beginning of a new way of thinking. The Laser's frame appeared to consist of smooth curves, but underneath it was tough and torsion-resistant.

The tubes were drop-shaped in cross-section, and in the most radical versions the components were not exposed to the wind but covered in the slipstream. Every detail speaks of precise, high-quality manufacture: the tubes had no lugs, the joints were lined with sheet metal and seams sanded down by hand. A Cinelli Laser (in this case number 029) is a work of art that can be ridden, with a price to match.

Cino Cinelli founded his company in 1947 and became legendary for his innovative ideas for cycle racing. When he retired in 1978, a new era dawned at the Cinelli company: the Colombo brothers (Colombus Tubing) bought the firm and Cino's son, Andrea, took on the marketing. The logo was changed and Gianni Gabella, the technical manager, was given unlimited scope to develop the Laser model.

The aim was for this model to break records. A prototype was shown in 1979 and the first production models were used at the 1983 Pan Am Games in Caracas. Soon afterwards the Laser was notching up a series of victories, leaving its dazed opponents trailing minutes behind.

There were even tandems and futuristic versions of the model, including the Rivoluzione Pista, which had no seat tube and a fully encased stem. Cinelli also produced commercially available editions for the road.

At the end of the 1980s Andrea Cinelli made his own ideas a reality with the Cinetica Giotto (page 74).

# CORIMA Cougar
## RIDING INTO THE RECORDS

**VARIETY**
RACING, SINGLESPEED

**COUNTRY**
FRANCE

**DATE**
1991

**WEIGHT**
8.9 KG (19.6 LB)

**FRAME**
VARNISHED CARBON,
56 CM (22 IN.) HIGH

**GEAR**
1, FIXED

**TYRES**
27 IN. TUBULAR

The Corima Cougar was a powerful, muscular track bike with extraordinary high ambitions. This one was produced in France for the 1992 Olympic Games in Barcelona.

The monocoque frame was composed of carbon – a lighter, more stable material important for a track bike. Each of these rare bicycles was precisely made to measure for the athlete, whereas competitors' carbon frames were offered in only a few sizes. Around 1,000 Corima Cougar framesets were produced in total, one of which was ridden by British cyclist Chris Boardman when he broke the world hour record in 1993.

A love of carbon can be traced back through the Corima company history. Founded by Pierre Martin and Jean-Marie Riffard in 1973, the company name is a shortened anagram of Cooperation Riffard Martin. From 1988 onwards they focused intensively on developing carbon parts, and soon they had everything that could make a bike both light and expensive, from disc wheels to the complete carbon product line.

# BIANCHI C-4 Project
## WHEN THE FUTURE WAS STILL YOUNG

**VARIETY**
RACING

**COUNTRY**
ITALY

**DATE**
c. 1988

**WEIGHT**
11.4 KG (25.1 LB)

**FRAME**
VARNISHED CARBON,
57.5 CM (22.6 IN.) HIGH

**GEARS**
2 × 8, DERAILLEUR
SHIMANO DURA-ACE

**BRAKES**
RIM SIDE PULL
SHIMANO DURA-ACE

**TYRES**
26 IN. TUBULAR (FRONT),
27 IN. TUBULAR (REAR)

The shape of the Bianchi C-4 Project model shown here seems comically athletic, its organically shaped carbon frame pointing to an active future.

The bike was the result of a collaboration between two Italian companies: F.I.V. Edoardo Bianchi S.p.A, founded in 1885, is the world's oldest bicycle-making company still in existence, and remains a legend today; and C-4, which was founded over one hundred years later by Marco Bonfanti, to realize his design ideas.

Success came quickly, with the resulting C-4 frames making their debut in cycling competitions from spring 1987, when the Bianchi racing team took part in the time trial of the Giro d'Italia (Cycling Tour of Italy) equipped with fork frames designed and produced by C-4. These frames were years ahead of their time with their characteristic components: the entire carbon monocoque, created using the most up-to-date NJC (No Joint Construction) technology then available, the frame without a saddle pipe, the adjustable seat pin for all dimensions with three unique frame sizes and the carbon monocoque front fork. Later, the idea was also taken off-road, as the C-4 (see page 58) shows.

The Bianchi C-4 Project models were usually equipped with Campagnolo Record components, though those on the model featured are by Shimano Dura-Ace, widely used today on racing bikes. Shimano appeared on the market at the start of the 1970s with road bike components. These at first imitated Campagnolo parts, but they soon became renowned for their innovative products (aerodynamic components, indexed shift levers and so on). Both Shimano and Campagnolo continue to strive for technical dominance over the competition.

# PUCH Mistral Ultima
## OCCASIONALLY
## A LEGEND

**VARIETY**
RACING

**COUNTRY**
AUSTRIA

**DATE**
1982

**WEIGHT**
10.5 KG (23.1 LB)

**FRAME**
VARNISHED STEEL, 56 CM (22 IN.) HIGH

**GEARS**
2 X 6, DERAILLEUR CAMPAGNOLO SUPER RECORD

**BRAKES**
RIM SIDE PULL CAMPAGNOLO SUPER RECORD

**TYRES**
27 IN. TUBULAR

Marketing experts gave the Austrian county of Styria the label 'Austria's Green Heart'; consequently the top model from the (formerly) Styrian Puch concern was green. The Mistral Ultima was the noblest version of the Mistral series, the Campagnolo Super Record components were the very finest, the Reynolds-531 tubes truly cult. The series version had Cinelli rawhide saddles and handlebars wrapped in the same leather, the VIP ensemble, at that time the mark of the most expensive kind of bike construction. And so that the cyclists would stand out sufficiently as ambassadors for the brand, Puch established a professional team.

What started in 1980 as Puch–Sem–Campagnolo with Didi Thurau and Rudi Altig, was called Puch–Wolber–Campagnolo in 1981, when Klaus-Peter Thaler, for instance, was also involved. Puch professional teams existed under different names until 1985, but the company was soon a shadow of its former self. In 1987 Puch's bicycle arm was sold to the Piaggio concern; a few years later it belonged to the Swedish sports equipment producer Monark, part of the Cycleurope group. Today Puch has landed again in Austria: Faber, an importer of Vespa scooters, has acquired the rights to the make, and work is currently underway on a range of products including an electric bike.

# MOULTON
## Speed S
RAPID STAINLESS
STEEL

**VARIETY**
RACING

**COUNTRY**
UNITED KINGDOM

**DATE**
1997

**WEIGHT**
10.3 KG (22.7 LB)

**FRAME**
STAINLESS STEEL,
48 CM (18,9 IN.) HIGH

**GEARS**
2 X 9, SHIMANO ULTEGRA

**BRAKES**
RIM SIDE PULL SHIMANO

**TYRES**
17 IN. WIRED

a brilliant rubber suspension system can be used everywhere, thanks to a transmission ratio suitable for both flat roads and climbing mountains. And the enamoured owner can certainly enjoy spending as many hours polishing this bike as many a motor car owner spends on his vehicle on a Saturday morning.

The Moulton Speed S was produced in a small series in the early 1990s and sold for the price of a mid-size used car.

Stainless steel is heavier than ordinary steel, which in turn is heavier than aluminium, carbon or titanium, but its elegant surface attracted the interest of British inventor Alex Moulton as a raw material for superior frames. A special brazing solder from aircraft construction was used to link the narrow tubes and a graceful, cleverly conceived construction method saved weight, as the 11 kilogrammes of the Moulton Speed S attest. This thoroughbred racing bike with

# FES
## RACING BIKES
## EAST BLOC STYLE

**VARIETY**
RACING

**COUNTRY**
GERMANY/EAST GERMANY

**DATE**
1987

**WEIGHT**
9.9 KG (21.8 LB)

**FRAME**
CARBON MONOCOQUE, 55 CM (21.7 IN.) HIGH

**GEARS**
2 X 8, DERAILLEUR SHIMANO DURA ACE

**BRAKES**
RIM SIDE PULL SHIMANO DURA ACE

**TYRES**
27 IN. TUBULAR

It may be difficult to imagine this FES among the grey streets and generally muted hues of the GDR, but that is where this racing bike came from – and it was, so to speak, on an official mission, like the Textima steel bikes before it. The East Berlin firm FES (Forschung und Entwicklung von Sportgeräten, or Research and Development of Sport Equipment) was set up to design suitable equipment for the country's sportsmen and women. Initially the programme consisted of canoes, racing sleds and bobsleds; the earliest FES concepts for the road were produced in 1987. First they developed carbon wheels for racing bicycles, then entire frames using a highly progressive monocoque construction system, of a kind that was still far from commonplace in the western racing scene. The FES frames, each manufactured for an elite cyclist, were not to be seen at professional races, as only amateur races were held in the GDR, and sportsmen and women from the country were allowed to travel to the West only for the Olympics. The Tour de France of the Eastern Bloc was the so-called Peace Race. However, GDR cyclists nonetheless reached world-class level, as proven by 16 medals at the Olympic Games.

The extremely western Shimano Dura Ace parts may not exactly fit the image, but strangely enough western components were acceptable in GDR racing. Perhaps the authorities relied on the fact that, as the bikes flashed by at high speeds, it was practically impossible to read the tiny labels.

The same could not be said of the start number, for which a fixing lug was mounted to the top tube. A start number often hung on the fine FES frame, even long after the end of the GDR – the futuristic frame outlived the backward state, and FES continues to research and develop down to the present day.

# GUERCIOTTI
## ITALY, QUITE
## CLEARLY

**VARIETY**
RACING

**COUNTRY**
ITALY

**DATE**
1987

**WEIGHT**
11 KG (24.2 LB)

**FRAME**
PAINTED STEEL, 53 CM (20.9 IN.) HIGH

**GEARS**
2 X 8, DERAILLEUR SHIMANO DURA ACE

**BRAKES**
RIM SIDE PULL SHIMANO DURA ACE

**TYRES**
28 IN. WIRED

Combining the Italian national colours in a bike frame was probably first introduced in the 1930s by Umberto Dei, but was far too logical an idea not to be copied by other manufacturers. By Gianni Motta for example, or by Guerciotti, where the attention given to detail is also extended to the lugs: slender parts with delicately meandering engravings indicate frame building of the finest kind, and the same level of art is applied to completing the frame with the colour concept continued to the rims, handlebar tape and saddle.

Guerciotti was founded in 1964 in Milan by the brothers Paolo and Italo Guerciotti, neither of them exactly new to bicycles: Paolo came from cyclo-cross, Italo from road racing, and it was Italo, the older of the two, who made the first frames.

Incidentally, this young firm received support from Cino Cinelli, who today is also a legend.

# ALAN
# Record Carbonio
## SOMETHING NEW
## FROM THE PIONEER

**VARIETY**
RACING

**COUNTRY**
ITALY

**DATE**
1987

**WEIGHT**
9.4 KG (20.7 LB)

**FRAME**
CARBON TUBES IN ALUMINIUM LUGS,
54 CM (21.3 IN.) HIGH

**GEARS**
2 X 6, DERAILLEUR CAMPAGNOLO CHORUS

**BRAKES**
RIM SIDE PULL CAMPAGNOLO CHORUS

**TYRES**
28 IN. WIRED

Two worlds encounter each other and are (still) peacefully united: in the mid-1980s Alan, an aluminium pioneer famous since 1972 for its comfortable racing and cross-country frame, entered the carbon age. This frame was not the future, however – the carbon tubes are bonded using aluminium lugs, whereas the nature of carbon demands the flowing transitions of a monocoque frame. Under loading, the bonded areas separated just as easily as one might suspect. But the beauty of this noble combination is still convincing today, at a time when carbon has largely replaced aluminium for racing bikes.

Klaus-Peter Thaler was world cyclo-cross champion several times on a legendary Alan aluminium frame. And the fact that the Alan Carbonio is so strikingly similar to the Colnago Carbitubo (see page 84) is largely because the latter was also produced by Alan.

271

# LOOK KG 196
# CARBON FOR
# WINNERS

**VARIETY**
RACING

**COUNTRY**
FRANCE

**DATE**
1996

**WEIGHT**
9.5 KG (20.9 LB)

**FRAME**
CARBON MONOCOQUE,
53 CM (20.9 IN.) HIGH

**GEARS**
2 X 7, DERAILLEUR SHIMANO DURA ACE

**BRAKES**
RIM SIDE PULL SHIMANO DURA ACE

**TYRES**
27 IN. TUBULAR

The firm LOOK originally made ski bindings, and came to bicycles by a roundabout route. Snap-on pedals were practically a by-product of their core business, but in 1986, one year after Bernard Hinault's Tour de France victory using LOOK pedals, they put their name to an entire bicycle. Greg Lemond, Hinault's great rival and a teammate in 1985, won the 1986 edition with a LOOK racing bike – the first Tour victory for a carbon frame and perhaps the catalyst for the research carried out by FES in East Berlin.

Ten years later, LOOK produced this time-trial machine, whose frame and chainstays evoke the shape of muscles. The steering recalls the neck steering on bicycles from the 1880s. The rest of the design is characterized by slightly detached fantasies of the future; only the back wheel can easily be retrieved from higher spheres – when the wind blows from the side, the cyclist struggles.

# TEXTIMA
# Time Trial
## DOWNHILL, YET UPHILL

**VARIETY**
RACING

**COUNTRY**
GERMANY/EAST GERMANY

**DATE**
1984

**WEIGHT**
8.6 KG (18.9 LB)

**FRAME**
PAINTED STEEL, 54 CM (21.3 IN.) HIGH

**GEARS**
2 X 6, DERAILLEUR CAMPAGNOLO SUPER RECORD

**BRAKES**
RIM SIDE PULL FRONT TEXTIMA,
REAR CAMPAGNOLO RECORD

**TYRES**
26 IN. WIRED

Textima was the name of the state textile machinery combine in the GDR, but the path to this excellent time trial bike is nevertheless a short one, if one thinks with the logic of the GDR. Although the cycle firm Diamant also belonged to Textima, which for the most part produced knitting machines, the department that developed racing bikes for top GDR sportsmen and women was integrated with the central testing department and had nothing to do with Diamant bikes.

To be precise the racing bikes were not even called Textima, but had no name at all. Names were very rarely found on the bicycles, but among collectors Textima today stands for the racing bike creations produced between 1975 and 1988 for the GDR national team by various special workshops in Leipzig and Chemnitz.

These bikes were never offered for sale: each of them was brazed and completed especially for a specific cyclist. The road racing bikes were blue, those for the track were silver, and the technology was among the best in the world: bladed spokes, especially hard and light magnesium wheel rims, extremely short chainstays, bespoke handlebars, aerodynamically oval or drop-shaped tubes and, naturally, the specially developed front wheel brake that was hidden from the airstream behind the fork. Towards the end of the GDR, Textima's technologies were overtaken by FES and its carbon creations; elite cyclists then obtained their sport equipment from East Berlin.

# MOSER
## Hour Record Replica
### LEANING FORWARD

**VARIETY**
SINGLESPEED, RACING

**COUNTRY**
ITALY

**DATE**
1984

**WEIGHT**
9.9 KG (21.8 LB)

**FRAME**
CHROMED STEEL, 54 CM (21.3 IN.) HIGH

**GEARS**
NONE

**BRAKES**
NONE

**TYRES**
27 IN. TUBULAR

After the end of their careers many racing cyclists moved into building bikes; in the case of Francesco Moser these two phases overlapped somewhat. Thus he was able to win races on bikes bearing his own name – and to break records on them. In 1984 in Mexico City, Francesco Moser set out to break Eddy Merckx´s 12-year-old hour record; a short time later the record was smashed with a figure of 50.808 km in one hour. Unsated, four days later Moser attempted to improve his own mark. The new world hour record of 51.151 km in an hour was to remain unbeaten for nine years.

After the world record, the Austrian racing cyclist Bernhard Rassinger, State Champion on the road at the Tour of Austria and 1987 bronze medallist at the road racing world championships in Villach, ordered a bicycle built to the exact same specifications from Francesco Moser in person. This is our photo model bike. Moser's record of 51.151 km/h was already engraved in the 3ttt handlebars.

# FAGGIN
## THE HIGHEST KIND OF ART

**VARIETY**
SINGLESPEED, RACING

**COUNTRY**
ITALY

**DATE**
1986

**WEIGHT**
8.9 KG (19.6 LB)

**FRAME**
PAINTED STEEL, 52 CM (20.5 IN.) HIGH

**GEARS**
NONE

**BRAKES**
NONE

**TYRES**
27 IN. TUBULAR

278

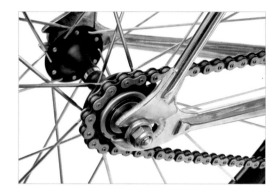

Faggin started as a bicycle manufacturer in 1945, and much has remained the same to the present day. Faggin frames are still regarded as works of art, lovingly put together by hand, checked and fine-tuned until every detail is right. Over the years a number of new frame materials have been used as fashions change and technology advances. Today there are Faggin bikes with carbon frames, but steel, the classic material for frame building, was never completely set aside in favour of newer technologies – even today two racing bikes, a single-speed bike and a touring bike are available with classic steel frames.

Faggin's track bike epitomizes the degree of love and care that goes into the tiniest part: the lugs are made with great attention to detail – where the seat tube and top tube meet there are even two – and the stem is engraved.

There are many Faggin bikes that one could gaze at in admiration for hours without even riding them, and in some cases one could almost look forever.

# ALEX SINGER
## GOD LIVES!

**VARIETY**
TOURING

**COUNTRY**
FRANCE

**DATE**
1947

**WEIGHT**
10.6 KG (23.3 LB)

**FRAME**
PAINTED STEEL, 57 CM (22.4 IN.) HIGH

**GEARS**
2 X 4, DERAILLEUR CYCLO

**BRAKES**
RIM CENTRE PULL SINGER

**TYRES**
26 IN. WIRED

At a time when, in many countries, touring bikes were still heavy and awkward, France perfected lightweight construction. From the mid-1930s onwards frame builders took part in randonneur competitions to find out who could build the lightest and yet most robust bike. Simply shedding weight was not enough: the rider had, after all, to reach his goal as fast as possible and with his luggage.

Alongside René Herse, Alex Singer is today regarded as one of the patron saints of French frame building and this bike shows why. In every fibre a loving attention to graceful, elegantly contrived details is evident: two thin screws are lighter than a thick one, so the saddle and the stem are joined with delicate double screws; the rear derailleur is attached to four ultra-thin tubes brazed to the frame, the front

derailleur consists solely of outlines formed by thin wire, and the delicate brakes can slow down even a well-laden machine.

In 1964, following Alex Singer's serious illness, his nephews Roland and Ernest Csuka took over the business, which they ran together until Roland died in 1993, leaving Ernest as sole head of Singer until 2009. Olivier, Ernest's son, continues the line today. Ernest was not just a gifted bicycle builder but also won two stages of the Tour de France Cyclotouriste in 1950, on a Singer Randonneur. In this competition the Tour stages were the same as for professional cyclists; the randonneurs were the first to pass the spectators, and in the cyclosportif class the last 50 kilometres were a race against each other and the clock.

# KETTLER ALU-RAD
## Strato
### ALUMINIUM TEARDROP

**VARIETY**
RACING

**COUNTRY**
GERMANY

**DATE**
1982

**WEIGHT**
10.9 KG (24 LB)

**FRAME**
ALUMINIUM, 57 CM (22.4 IN.) HIGH

**GEARS**
2 X 6, DERAILLEUR SHIMANO 600 AX

**BRAKES**
RIM CENTRE PULL SHIMANO 600 AX

**TYRES**
27 IN. TUBULAR

Kettler made aluminium frames more affordable, and the results are clearly visible in most of their bikes. Where you might expect to see polished aluminium, Kettler frames were simply painted silver and the intricate detailing was also dropped. Aerodynamics were still a priority, though: the tubes that make up this frame have a teardrop-shaped cross-section and even the fork head is slightly streamlined, although the frame and fork retain a characteristic solidity.

The Shimano 600 AX components, however, are graceful and elegant; every detail is made with the precision for which Shimano has always been known. The oversized pedal threads are positioned above the tread surface so as to extend the crank arm, the brakes are wonderfully aerodynamic, and even the saddle stem with its internal clamping is aerodynamically optimized.

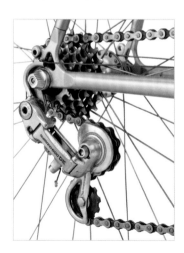

# CESARE M
## THE MARK
## OF QUALITY

**VARIETY**
RACING

**COUNTRY**
ITALY

**DATE**
1989

**WEIGHT**
9.9 KG (21.8 LB)

**FRAME**
CHROMED STEEL, 52 CM (20.5 IN.) HIGH

**GEARS**
2 X 8, DERAILLEUR CAMPAGNOLO RECORD

**BRAKES**
RIM CENTRE PULL CAMPAGNOLO DELTA

**TYRES**
28 IN. WIRED

Long before the internet age, bike parts could be ordered by post and a hefty Brügelmann catalogue was the cyclist's bible. The German mail order firm still exists today, but its house brand Cesare M only survives on fine racing bikes like this one. The way the rear brake cable is led through the top tube is typical of the firm's attention to detail, and the point where the seat stays meet the saddle clamp is beautiful, as are the Campagnolo Delta brakes matched to the Shamal wheels. In fact, the lightweight construction led to rims so thin that they would deform under emergency braking, so the Deltas were specified because they could not build up enough friction to cause damage. Cesare M frames were welded in Italy, where the earlier house brand Barellia was also made, but there was never any mention of a specific designer called Cesare M in the Brügelmann catalogue.

# BIANCHI
# Rekord 746
## THE COLOUR
## OF CLASS

**VARIETY**
RACING

**COUNTRY**
ITALY

**DATE**
1980

**WEIGHT**
12.4 KG (27.3 LB)

**FRAME**
PAINTED STEEL, 58 CM (22.8 IN.) HIGH

**GEARS**
2 X 5, DERAILLEUR CAMPAGNOLO
NUOVO RECORD

**BRAKES**
RIM SIDE PULL GALLI

**TYRES**
27 IN. TUBULAR

The colour that has become synonymous with this marque is often called Bianchi Green, but its official name, 'celeste', sounds a little classier and suits this rare bike. The question of how celeste first came to be the colour of Bianchi frames is an old one and tricky to answer. Several ideas have been suggested, although only one can be correct. Here is a small selection: Edoardo Bianchi chose celeste in honour of Queen Margherita of Italy, to match the colour of her eyes; the shade was an homage to the sky over Milan; there was a mistake with colour mixing before the Giro but no time to repaint the frames. However, the claim that the colour was created by mixing leftover blue and green paint after the Second World War can be discounted, because Bianchi were already using celeste by the late 1890s. Perhaps the most plausible theory is that Bianchi wanted his racers in a colour that nobody else in the starting field would be using.

To this day, Bianchi is to cycling what Ferrari is to motorsport: a high-speed legend. Nevertheless, not all its road bikes are as enchantingly elegant as this 746. To make the spirit of the brand more affordable, Bianchi brought the model down a few price points and fans eagerly snapped it up.

# GIOS
# Aerodynamic
## THE HIGHEST END

**VARIETY**
RACING

**COUNTRY**
ITALY

**DATE**
1981

**WEIGHT**
9.4 KG (20.7 LB)

**FRAME**
PAINTED STEEL, 55 CM (21.7 IN.) HIGH

**GEARS**
2 X 6, DERAILLEUR CAMPAGNOLO RECORD

**BRAKES**
RIM SIDE PULL DIA COMPE

**TYRES**
27 IN. TUBULAR

Like many cyclists, Tolmino Gios started producing bicycles soon after he stopped racing professionally, in 1948, and the brand has remained in family hands to the present day, with his son Alfredo now at its head.

It was chewing gum, however, that made Gios racing bikes into legends. If Giorgio Perfetti (who could go wrong with a name like that?), owner of the Italian chewing gum brand Brooklyn, had not ordered a hundred Gios Easy Rider bikes at the 1971 Milan Cycling Show, then he might never have set up a professional cycling team and Gios might have been forgotten. Gios equipped the team with paintwork to match its stars-and-stripes jerseys, creating a striking image. Since then, all Gios racing bikes have sported this simple mid-blue, which is now known as 'Gios Blue', having carried winners such as Roger de Vlaeminck and Didi Thurau. Today the most famous Gios racing bikes are the Professional and this one, the Aerodynamic.

Since 2011, a model with very slender steel frame tubes and chromed lugs – the Gios Compact Pro – has been available once again, a legend revisited that has made a splash on the growing retro market.

# COLNAGO
## Oval CX
## RESISTANCE
## IS FUTILE

**VARIETY**
RACING

**COUNTRY**
ITALY

**DATE**
1983

**WEIGHT**
9.9 KG (21.8 LB)

**FRAME**
PAINTED STEEL, 57 CM (22.4 IN.) HIGH

**GEARS**
2 X 6, DERAILLEUR CAMPAGNOLO SUPER RECORD

**BRAKES**
RIM SIDE PULL CAMPAGNOLO COBALTO

**TYRES**
28 IN. WIRED

No body can ever be as aerodynamic as a teardrop, but the nearest a road bike can get is tubes with a teardrop-shaped cross-section. Although the wind resistance of the rider remains the major weak point (much greater than that of the frame), aero frames became very popular in the early eighties – in a sense, they gave an aerodynamic feel, even if they were powerless against the laws of physics.

In the early eighties, Colnago was already a cult brand, and the combination of the brand and the aero profile made it nothing less than legendary. The Oval CX was lovingly detailed down to the last bolt; the seat tube cluster alone is a work of art, the rear brake is mounted on the inside, to keep it out of the wind, there are engravings at several points on the frame, and everything is so effortless that the Oval CX could practically pass as a sculpture. An awestruck silence is the only suitable reaction.

# GLOSSARY

**Aero spokes (bladed spokes)**
Spokes that are not round, but oblong in cross-section.

**Bicycle rollers**
A device with three rollers, which can be used to cycle on the spot.

**Bottom bracket**
Shaft to which the cranks are connected, together with their ball bearings and bearing shells.

**Campagnolo**
Italian manufacturer of racing bike components, steeped in history. Enjoys a cult following among many cycling fans.

**Cantilever brake**
A brake with two small pivot levers, on the left and right of the fork and on the **seat stays**. The levers are fastened to brazed-on pivot points.

**Chain ring**
The front toothed wheel on which the chain runs.

**Chain stays**
The two thin tubes between the bottom bracket and the rear drop-outs (a type of fork-end that enables the rear wheel to be removed without derailing the chain first).

**Coaster brake**
A brake mounted in the rear wheel hub. It is activated by pedalling in the opposite direction.

**Cranks**
The arm that connects the pedal to the bottom bracket axle. The cranks are rotated by the rider, and the pedals and the chain ring are fastened to the cranks.

**Cross frame**
A frame consisting of two (usually thick) crossed tubes.

**Derailleur (front and rear)**
Adopted from the French and meaning the gear mechanism. It enables the rider to move the chain from one sprocket to another, and so change gears. A distinction is made between the front derailleur (at the chain ring) and the rear derailleur because they look dissimilar and work in different ways.

**Diamond frame**
The classic frame shape, with four tubes connected to form a trapezium at its centre.

**Disc brake**
A brake in which linings are pressed against a steel disc, fastened to the wheel hub.

**Disc wheel**
A wheel formed from a solid, continuous disc instead of spokes.

**Drum brake**
A brake mounted in the hub, with its linings pressed against the drum from the inside.

**Dura-Ace**
Shimano's best and most expensive racing bike components.

**Electronic gears**
A gear system operated electronically rather than by means of a Bowden cable.

**Floating axle**
An axle occasionally used in the rear wheel. It can be removed from the bicycle without loosening any screws.

**Frame height** (German/Italian)
The height of a frame must be suited to the rider's leg length. In Italy the frame is measured from the centre of the bottom bracket axle to the centre of the top tube. However, in Germany – and virtually every other country – the frame is measured from the centre of the bottom bracket axle to the top edge of the seat lug.

**Head tube**
The tube in which the fork rotates.

**Hetchins Magnum Opus**
The top-of-the-range model from Hetchins, famous as one of the greatest lightweights. It is distinguished by its particularly ornately filed lugs.

**Hub**
Components in the centre of the front and rear wheels. The hub rotates around the axle.

**Linkage brake (rod brake)**
A brake in which the braking force is transmitted via a linkage or rod system (and not by means of a Bowden cable).

**Lugs**
Components for connecting the individual frame tubes.

**Monocoque frame**
A frame produced as a single piece, not individual tubes.

**Quick-release mechanism**
A mechanism that runs through the hub axle, enabling the wheel to be removed or attached by turning a lever.

**Randonneur**
A randonneur is a type of French touring bicycle, dating from the early 20th century.

**Rear stays**
The seat stays and chain stays together form the rear frame.

**Seat clamp bolt**
The bolt used to fix the seatpost at the desired height.

**Seat stays**
The two thin tubes between the seat lug and the rear drop-outs (see above: **chain stays**).

**Seat stay bridge**
A small connecting piece of the frame between the seat stays, in which the rear brake is mounted.

**Seat tube**
The tube between the bottom bracket and the seat lug – that is, the tube in which the seatpost is fitted.

**Shimano**
A Japanese manufacturer of components – the world's leading manufacturer in its field.

**Single-speed, fixed-gear or fixed-wheel**
A wheel that is permanently fixed to the sprocket on the rear hub. This means the rider must pedal at all times while the bike is moving.

**Super Record**
The best and most expensive racing bike components made by Campagnolo, an Italian bicycle manufacturer. They were produced between 1975 and 1986, and again since 2009.

**Tubular**
A type of racing bike tyre in which the inner tube and tyre casing are adhesively bonded to the rim as a single unit.

**Tyre dimensions**
A tyre's dimensions are provided by its diameter and thickness. The measurement in inches usually gives the external diameter, while the measurement in millimetres usually relates to the inside of the tyre where it meets the rim.

**V-brake**
A brake that is practically the successor of the cantilever brake. The levers are longer and point nearly vertically upwards, which means that the cable has a more direct effect.

**Wheelbase**
The distance between the axle of the front and rear wheels.

**Wired tyre**
A type of tyre into which wire hoops are integrated to guarantee it stays on the rim.

# STATISTICS

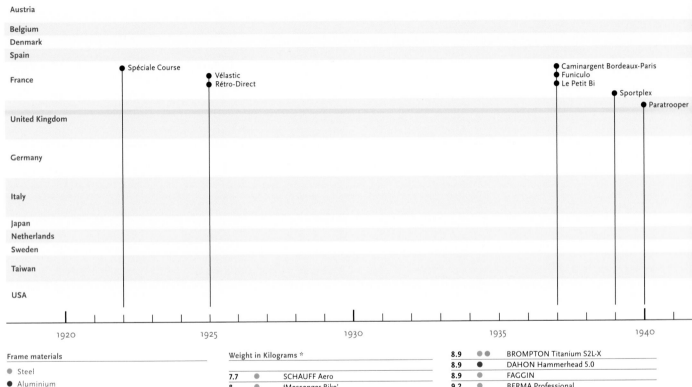

| | | | |
|---|---|---|---|
| Austria | | | |
| Belgium | | | |
| Denmark | | | |
| Spain | | | |
| France | ● Spéciale Course | ● Vélastic<br>● Rétro-Direct | ● Caminargent Bordeaux-Paris<br>● Funiculo<br>● Le Petit Bi<br>● Sportplex<br>● Paratrooper |
| United Kingdom | | | |
| Germany | | | |
| Italy | | | |
| Japan | | | |
| Netherlands | | | |
| Sweden | | | |
| Taiwan | | | |
| USA | | | |

1920     1925     1930     1935     1940

**Frame materials**

- ● Steel
- ● Aluminium
- ● Carbon
- ● Magnesium
- ● Plastic
- ● Titanium

\* For weights in imperial units (lb),
please refer to the technical specifications
given in each bicycle entry

**Weight in Kilograms \***

| | | |
|---|---|---|
| 7.7 | ● | SCHAUFF Aero |
| 8 | ● | 'Messenger Bike' |
| 8.2 | ● | SELECT Campionissimo |
| 8.2 | ● ● | COLNAGO Carbitubo Pista |
| 8.3 | ● | CAMINADE Caminargent Bordeaux-Paris |
| 8.5 | ● | SABLIÈRE |
| 8.5 | ● | MERCIAN 'Custom' |
| 8.6 | ● | TEXTIMA Time Trial |
| 8.7 | ● | INBIKE/TEXTIMA |
| 8.9 | ● | CORIMA Cougar |

| | | |
|---|---|---|
| 8.9 | ● ● | BROMPTON Titanium S2L-X |
| 8.9 | ● | DAHON Hammerhead 5.0 |
| 8.9 | ● | FAGGIN |
| 9.2 | ● | BERMA Professional |
| 9.2 | ● | C. B. T. ITALIA Champions |
| 9.3 | ● | CYCLES GITANE Profil Aero TT |
| 9.3 | ● | 3RENSHO Super Record Export |
| 9.3 | ● | GT Vengeance Aero Mark Allen Edition |
| 9.4 | ● | COLNAGO Brügelmann |
| 9.4 | ● ● | ALAN RECORD Carbonio |
| 9.4 | ● | GIOS Aerodynamic |
| 9.5 | ● | CINELLI Laser |

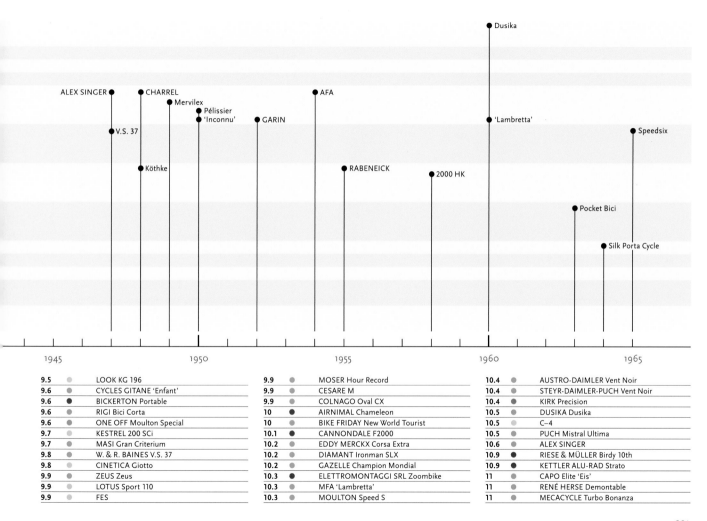

Dusika

ALEX SINGER ●    ● CHARREL              ● AFA

● Mervilex

● V.S. 37        ● Pélissier            'Lambretta'        ● Speedsix
                  'Inconnu'
                              ● GARIN

● Köthke                                ● RABENEICK       ● 2000 HK

                                        ● Pocket Bici

                                        ● Silk Porta Cycle

1945            1950            1955            1960            1965

| | | | |
|---|---|---|---|
| **9.5** ● LOOK KG 196 | **9.9** ● MOSER Hour Record | **10.4** ● AUSTRO-DAIMLER Vent Noir | |
| **9.6** ● CYCLES GITANE 'Enfant' | **9.9** ● CESARE M | **10.4** ● STEYR-DAIMLER-PUCH Vent Noir | |
| **9.6** ● BICKERTON Portable | **9.9** ● COLNAGO Oval CX | **10.4** ● KIRK Precision | |
| **9.6** ● RIGI Bici Corta | **10** ● AIRNIMAL Chameleon | **10.5** ● DUSIKA Dusika | |
| **9.6** ● ONE OFF Moulton Special | **10** ● BIKE FRIDAY New World Tourist | **10.5** ● C–4 | |
| **9.7** ● KESTREL 200 SCi | **10.1** ● CANNONDALE F2000 | **10.5** ● PUCH Mistral Ultima | |
| **9.7** ● MASI Gran Criterium | **10.2** ● EDDY MERCKX Corsa Extra | **10.6** ● ALEX SINGER | |
| **9.8** ● W. & R. BAINES V.S. 37 | **10.2** ● DIAMANT Ironman SLX | **10.9** ● RIESE & MÜLLER Birdy 10th | |
| **9.8** ● CINETICA Giotto | **10.2** ● GAZELLE Champion Mondial | **10.9** ● KETTLER ALU-RAD Strato | |
| **9.9** ● ZEUS Zeus | **10.3** ● ELETTROMONTAGGI SRL Zoombike | **11** ● CAPO Elite 'Eis' | |
| **9.9** ● LOTUS Sport 110 | **10.3** ● MFA 'Lambretta' | **11** ● RENÉ HERSE Demontable | |
| **9.9** ● FES | **10.3** ● MOULTON Speed S | **11** ● MECACYCLE Turbo Bonanza | |

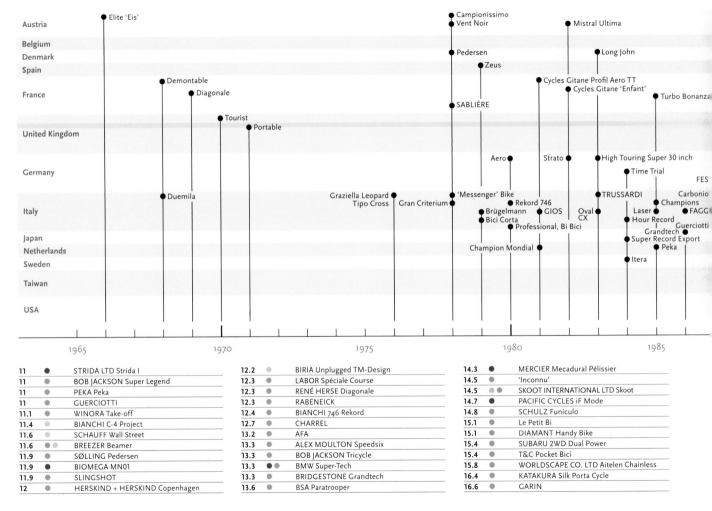

| 11 | • | STRIDA LTD Strida I |
|---|---|---|
| 11 | • | BOB JACKSON Super Legend |
| 11 | • | PEKA Peka |
| 11 | • | GUERCIOTTI |
| 11.1 | • | WINORA Take-off |
| 11.4 | • | BIANCHI C-4 Project |
| 11.6 | • | SCHAUFF Wall Street |
| 11.6 | •• | BREEZER Beamer |
| 11.9 | • | SØLLING Pedersen |
| 11.9 | • | BIOMEGA MN01 |
| 11.9 | • | SLINGSHOT |
| 12 | • | HERSKIND + HERSKIND Copenhagen |

| 12.2 | • | BIRIA Unplugged TM-Design |
|---|---|---|
| 12.3 | • | LABOR Spéciale Course |
| 12.3 | • | RENÉ HERSE Diagonale |
| 12.3 | • | RABENEICK |
| 12.4 | • | BIANCHI 746 Rekord |
| 12.7 | • | CHARREL |
| 13.2 | • | AFA |
| 13.3 | • | ALEX MOULTON Speedsix |
| 13.3 | • | BOB JACKSON Tricycle |
| 13.3 | •• | BMW Super-Tech |
| 13.3 | • | BRIDGESTONE Grandtech |
| 13.6 | • | BSA Paratrooper |

| 14.3 | • | MERCIER Mecadural Pélissier |
|---|---|---|
| 14.5 | • | 'Inconnu' |
| 14.5 | •• | SKOOT INTERNATIONAL LTD Skoot |
| 14.7 | • | PACIFIC CYCLES iF Mode |
| 14.8 | • | SCHULZ Funiculo |
| 15.1 | • | Le Petit Bi |
| 15.1 | • | DIAMANT Handy Bike |
| 15.4 | • | SUBARU 2WD Dual Power |
| 15.4 | • | T&C Pocket Bici |
| 15.8 | • | WORLDSCAPE CO. LTD Aitelen Chainless |
| 16.4 | • | KATAKURA Silk Porta Cycle |
| 16.6 | • | GARIN |

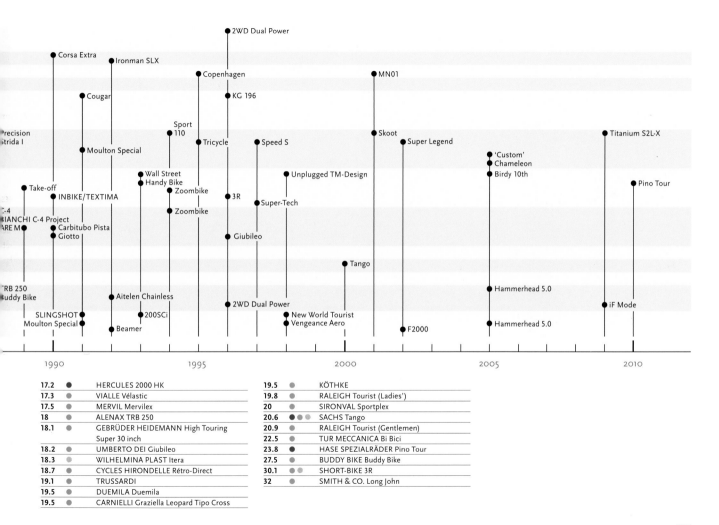

2WD Dual Power

Corsa Extra

Ironman SLX

Cougar

Copenhagen

MN01

KG 196

Precision
Strida I

Sport
110

Skoot

Titanium S2L-X

Moulton Special

Tricycle

Speed S

Super Legend

'Custom'
Chameleon

Birdy 10th

Wall Street
Handy Bike

Unplugged TM-Design

Pino Tour

Take-off

Zoombike

INBIKE/TEXTIMA

3R

C-4
BIANCHI C-4 Project
ARE M

Zoombike

Super-Tech

Carbitubo Pista
Giotto

Giubileo

Tango

TRB 250
Buddy Bike

Aitelen Chainless

Hammerhead 5.0

iF Mode

SLINGSHOT
Moulton Special

200SCi

2WD Dual Power

New World Tourist
Vengeance Aero

F2000

Hammerhead 5.0

Beamer

1990                    1995                    2000                    2005                    2010

| 17.2 | ● | HERCULES 2000 HK |
|---|---|---|
| 17.3 | ● | VIALLE Vélastic |
| 17.5 | ● | MERVIL Mervilex |
| 18 | ● | ALENAX TRB 250 |
| 18.1 | ● | GEBRÜDER HEIDEMANN High Touring Super 30 inch |
| 18.2 | ● | UMBERTO DEI Giubileo |
| 18.3 | ● | WILHELMINA PLAST Itera |
| 18.7 | ● | CYCLES HIRONDELLE Rétro-Direct |
| 19.1 | ● | TRUSSARDI |
| 19.5 | ● | DUEMILA Duemila |
| 19.5 | ● | CARNIELLI Graziella Leopard Tipo Cross |

| 19.5 | ● | KÖTHKE |
|---|---|---|
| 19.8 | ● | RALEIGH Tourist (Ladies') |
| 20 | ● | SIRONVAL Sportplex |
| 20.6 | ● ● ● | SACHS Tango |
| 20.9 | ● | RALEIGH Tourist (Gentlemen) |
| 22.5 | ● | TUR MECCANICA Bi Bici |
| 23.8 | ● | HASE SPEZIALRÄDER Pino Tour |
| 27.5 | ● | BUDDY BIKE Buddy Bike |
| 30.1 | ● ● | SHORT-BIKE 3R |
| 32 | ● | SMITH & CO. Long John |

MICHAEL EMBACHER
IS A DESIGNER AND ARCHITECT WHO HAS ASSEMBLED ONE OF THE WORLD'S GREATEST
COLLECTIONS OF BICYCLES. HE LIVES IN VIENNA, AUSTRIA.

PAUL SMITH
IS A WORLD-FAMOUS FASHION DESIGNER AND A PASSIONATE CYCLIST.

THE AUTHOR WOULD LIKE SINCERELY
TO THANK THE FOLLOWING PEOPLE:

YING-SHAN SCHWEIZER-EMBACHER
FOR BEING THE ENERGY SOURCE IN MY LIFE AND THE
MOST IMPORTANT SOURCE OF SUPPORT IN MAKING
THIS BOOK BECOME A REALITY.

BERNHARD ANGERER
WHOSE PHOTOGRAPHS MAKE THE BICYCLES TRULY
SPARKLE.

LUCAS DIETRICH
FOR BEING AN UNTIRING CHAMPION OF THIS BOOK.

ALEXANDER MEIXNER
FOR HIS INDEFATIGABLE SUPPORT, WHICH MADE IT
POSSIBLE TO COMPILE THIS COLLECTION IN THE
FIRST PLACE.

AS WELL AS
ANSGAR AMMERMANN, KLEMENS BILZER, JÜRGEN
BORGMANN, BENEDIKT CROY, MEINRAD FIXL, CAT
GLOVER, ROMAN GOLD, SANDRA GUGIC, FRANZ HAGER,
FRANZ HAMEDL, SEN. & JUN., KARIN HIRSCHBERGER,
GERALD & JUTTA LEVINSKY, ALEXANDER MARCH,
STEFAN MEIXNER, ISABEL NEUDHART, JOSEF PERNDL,
GERHARD PICHLER, DANIEL REINHARTZ, HERBERT RISTL,
STEFAN SCHAEFFER, BRIGITTE SCHEDL-RICHTER,
DIETRICH SCHMIDT, WALTER SCHMIEDL, MARIE-LOUISE
SCHWEIZER, HANSPETER SIGRIST, JAKOB STALDER,
RUPERT STEINER, MARTIN STRUBREITER, MARTIN
WAGNER, HEINRICH WALTER, RENÉ WINKLER, MICHAEL
ZAPPE, FRIEDRICH ZAUNRIETH.

SPECIAL THANKS
LIESELOTTE, GOTTFRIED AND VINCENZ EMBACHER

COVER DESIGN
PHOTOGRAPHS BY BERNHARD ANGERER

TEXT PREPARATION
JUTTA LEVINSKY, STEFAN MEIXNER, MARIE-LOUISE
SCHWEIZER, YING-SHAN SCHWEIZER-EMBACHER

TRANSLATION FROM THE GERMAN
BRAINSTORM, RODERICK O'DONOVAN
JILL PHYTHIAN (FINAL 5 ENTRIES)

PICTURE CREDITS
ALL PHOTOGRAPHS © 2011 AND 2019 BERNHARD
ANGERER, EXCEPT FOR THE FOLLOWING:
PAGE 7 © 2011 AND 2019 DANIEL STIER
PAGE 9 © 2011 AND 2019 ANDREAS MÜLLER

Published in 2019 in the United States
of America by Thames & Hudson Inc.,
500 Fifth Avenue, New York, New York 10110

www.thamesandhudsonusa.com

A previous edition under the same title
was published in 2011 in the United States
of America by Chronicle Books.

Library of Congress Control Number
2018956159

ISBN 978-0-500-29397-3

Printed and bound in China by C&C Offset
Printing Co. Ltd